Where After

WHERE do our loved ones go
AFTER they die?

Where After

WHERE do our loved ones go
AFTER they die?

Mariel Forde Clarke

6TH
BOOKS

Winchester, UK
Washington, USA

JOHN HUNT PUBLISHING

First published by Sixth Books, 2021
Sixth Books is an imprint of John Hunt Publishing Ltd., No. 3 East St., Alresford,
Hampshire SO24 9EE, UK
office@jhpbooks.com
www.johnhuntpublishing.com
www.6th-books.com

For distributor details and how to order please visit the 'Ordering' section on our website.

Text copyright: Mariel Forde Clarke 2020

ISBN: 978 1 78904 617 5
978 1 78904 618 2 (ebook)
Library of Congress Control Number: 2020939168

A CIP catalogue record for this book is available from the British Library.

Design: Stuart Davies

UK: Printed and bound by CPI Group (UK) Ltd, Croydon, CR0 4YY
Printed in North America by CPI GPS partners

We operate a distinctive and ethical publishing philosophy in
all areas of our business, from our global network of authors to
production and worldwide distribution.

Contents

Preface

There is an old Irish cliché that states, *"Life is a bitch and then you die."* Surely there must be more to life, a reason, a meaning as to why I was born, who am I and what happens when I die. My quest for such answers came in 1992 when I was diagnosed with cervical cancer and was facing my own mortality. I died on the operating table and found myself floating into a most magnificent light-filled space. Peace and tranquility enveloped me, and I felt at one with a presence that I had never known before. A universal love held me in sacredness as a Godhead energy of total bliss surrounded me. I had no fear as love and light enfolded me. Upon waking I felt little pain, the feeling of peace and tranquility caressed my body. I supposed the infusion of morphine was working its magic and helping paint my world in a kaleidoscope of color. Days later, I was informed by my surgeon that my surgery was extensive – I had died on the operating table while bleeding outwards. He said I was one lucky lady to be alive and that *"someone must have been watching over me."* My father died the year previous and I have no doubt he petitioned a Divine dispensation in my favor. I dedicated the following year to my recovery and healing, but the presence of this magnificent light never left me, it became my friend and constant companion. I understood then that there was a reason for my existence, but I needed to discover why.

The promise of a place, a heaven, was something I needed to explore. I became a seeker of knowledge. I explored different cultures ranging from Hinduism, Buddhism, Christianity and many more traditions that will be discussed later. I became a sponge for knowledge; I had an insatiable thirst for what lies beyond. I read many books on death and dying, I travelled abroad to undertake workshops. I studied many healing modalities, became a Shaman, an angel healer, crystal healer, grief counselor and teacher on spiritual awakening. I met amazing and inspiring teachers on my journey; to mention a few, Louise Hay, Marianne Williamson, Deepak Chopra, Dr. Brian Weiss, Wayne Dyer and many more. I studied Mediumship with the awesome James Van Praagh. I was only scratching the surface of what lies beyond the physical world beyond the five senses. Through my healing work I was receiving messages from people who had passed on. I was sensing blockages within the energy body of clients. I was beginning to understand that a powerful energy was guiding me and working through me. This energy I knew was not the energy I was born with, but a spiritual energy that would enter me when I invoked it prior to working on a client. Helen Keller once said that, *"The best and most beautiful things in the world cannot be seen or even touched. They must be felt with the heart."* I finally understood what her statement meant: during healing sessions I was transported onto a different plane of existence, where a download of Divine energy would seal me and a loving presence would over light the entire session. I was merely a channel, a conduit for this energy to pass through me. Was this the same light that people reported after having a near-death experience (NDE); was this the light I saw all those years earlier? I had to know, I craved the answers and they came in many different ways. It is only fitting to pay tribute to a number of inspirational studies and their authors while undertaking extensive research for the purpose of this book.

I have come to the conclusion that there will never be a definitive book on what happens when we die, which I think is good because no single book will ever convince skeptics or console everyone who has wondered about an afterlife. What might change society's fear and doubt is the rise of evidence put forward by scientists, doctors, professors, quantum physicists and many more who endorse the evidence that life continues after death.

Swedenborg (1668) known throughout the world as a genius provided many revelations in the exploration and mystery of the afterlife. A Swedish scientist, mathematician, statesman, inventor, author and mystic, at the age of 55 years he had a series of clairvoyant visions, which he said *"gave him the ability to experience the spiritual dimensions."* He claimed to have conversed with biblical prophets, apostles, Aristotle, Socrates and Caesar, as well as numerous deceased friends and acquaintances and spirits from other planets. He published thirty books, reporting on his explorations of the spirit world, including his conversations with many souls on the other side of the veil. In his first great work, *Arcana Coelestia*, he addressed the issue of life after death by writing: *"That I might know that man lives after death, it has been granted me to speak and converse with several persons with whom I had been acquainted during their life in the body, and this not merely for a day or a week, but for months, and in some instances for nearly a year, as I had been used to doing here on earth."* The most significant discovery by Swedenborg was the existence of a continuation of life beyond physical death.

Among the most influential researchers was the renowned Dr. Elisabeth Kübler-Ross who came under siege with the introduction of her first book *On Death and Dying* (1969). Kübler-Ross was ridiculed and laughed at by her medical colleagues. The idea that life continued after death was deemed absurd and ignorant. Years later the groundbreaking work of Dr. Raymond Moody (1975) opened up a whole new approach to the scientific understanding on Near-Death Experiences (NDEs). The studies of Moody on NDEs had astonishing findings, patients describing leaving their bodies, floating above their beds, watching doctors as they tried to restart their hearts, moving higher and being drawn towards a bright light, seeing a loved one and hearing them say, *"It's not your time."* The best clinical study on NDE was undertaken by Dutch cardiologist Dr. Pim van Lommel. He was astonished by commonalities in his findings, his patients were having vivid recall of life continuing after all neural activity ceased and were clinically pronounced dead. Dr. Penny Sartori, in *The Wisdom of Near-Death Experiences* (2014), states that NDEs undoubtedly occur and have very real, often dramatic, life-changing aftereffects. The results of her hospital research and that of others could not find a physiological or psychological explanation for these experiences, and indicated that they could no longer be ignored or explained away. Melvin Morse a pediatric doctor contributed excellent books and medical journals about the near-death experiences of children. His most renowned books are *Closer to the Light* (1990) and *Transformed by the Light* (1992). His findings showed that children who experienced near-death experiences had more meaningful, positive and fulfilling lives. He also found these children to have a higher rate of verifiable psychic abilities than those who had not experienced a near-death experience. Dr. George Ritchie (1950s) exposed himself to ridicule when he spoke openly about his own near-death experience. Ritchie was rejected by his medical cohort similar to Dr. Elisabeth Kübler-Ross and Dr. Moody when they endorsed the concept of near-death experience adding substance to proof of an afterlife. I was blessed to discover the renowned Irish author Colm Keane published many books containing comprehensive insights into Deathbed Visions: *We'll Meet Again*, *Going Home*, *The Distant Shore*, including the latest scientific research into what happens when we die. My most intriguing research was that of Dr. Victor Zammit, a retired attorney of the Supreme Court of Australia. After much research he has devoted the last twenty years to endorsing afterlife existence through scientific and medical research, *A Lawyer Presents the Case for the Afterlife*. So compelling the evidence, Zammit has offered one million dollars to anyone who can disprove an afterlife does not exist. To date no one has taken up this challenge.

In practically all studies examining the phenomenon of life after death, near-death experiences embody an overwhelming feeling of bliss, joy, tranquility, freedom, happiness, perfect health, a presence, being held in an eternal embrace where only pure love survives. I was fascinated by *The Tibetan Book of the Dead* as it contained centuries of religious practices in preparation for the onward journey and the interval between life and rebirth. I cast my net deeper and wider into other phenomenon, out-of-body experiences (OBEs), life after physical death, journey of the Soul, the afterlife, suicide, reincarnation and many more interrelated topics. All which will be shared throughout this book including the primary stages of grief, as well as powerful affirmations and messages from your loved one in spirit. To make reading this book more experiential, most chapters contain exercises intended to bring you closer to the world of spirit in a gentle and safe way. My purpose in writing this book is to offer a new way of thinking about death with scientific evidence to support an afterlife. It is my sincere wish that this book will shine a light of hope into the hearts and minds of its readers thus providing a compelling argument that beyond the darkness of death the soul rises immortal.

Foreword

You have within your hands an exceptional, deeply healing book which I trust will touch many far and wide.

The whole book is imbued with a deep love and gentle compassion which reflect the very essence of its author who could not write the way she does unless she lived it. She really walks her talk. It is from A to Z entirely based on the lived professional and personal experiences of Mariel, which is one of its main strengths. For in our world, there is such a great deal of speculation and theorizing about the afterlife. But here, no abstract musings – just the real thing if I may say. This is one of the main strengths of her message. The book is also the result of an intense and deeply sincere search for truth. As Mariel herself writes, "My faith in God has always been unshakable, but unless I've seen, touched, felt and experienced the details about how the whole creation of His works, I take absolutely nothing for granted and keep digging for answers." What integrity in such an approach – an integrity which pervades the whole book. And how reassuring for the reader: no fluffy musings in these pages, just authentic real life experiences.

The book replies in a simple and very direct manner to most of the questions people have concerning the afterlife and contacts with those who have passed on: are they really possible; is it not some figment of the imagination? For me, who had imagined that I was not a certified ignoramus on these questions, it was a profound and exciting learning experience.

Above all, the book is incredibly comforting and reassuring. It is from the first to the last page infused with the profound and powerful sense that, yes, we do live in an incredibly benevolent universe. That the Godhead (and you will put behind that term the words that have true significance for you: Infinite love, the Source, whatever) wants our well-being more than we could wish it for ourselves. That it protects and guides us whatever the apparent material picture, e.g. that of close relatives or friends who have left us via traumatic or disturbing events. This reassurance percolates gently through practically every page of the book and leaves the reader with a sense of deep wonder and gratitude: can it really be true that we live in such a fabulous universe? Yes, replies the author with an authority which undergirds the whole book.

An important section – important for a culture so immersed in the scientific approach to reality as ours – is the section on scientific evidence which upholds the phenomenon of NDEs (Near-Death Experiences) and especially the afterlife. And once more, you will never find any abstract theorizing, just one concrete example after the other, many of them experiences by the author or of one of the persons she was assisting in the grieving process.

Personally, the section that touched me most was the one on suicide. For a country like Ireland from which the author stems and where, due to the dominant religious teaching, those who depart via suicide are cruelly rejected and condemned, how comforting for those they leave behind to discover that on the other side there is not the slightest stigma or condemnation of the departed, but that they are welcomed with rejoicing, unconditional love and the deepest compassion. It is so deeply healing (as is the whole message of these pages). You will find an especially moving and helpful passage on how to be with loved ones when someone has committed suicide. This section is not only psychologically grounded but equally metaphysically very sound. Too often family and friends torture themselves with thoughts such as "if only I had done (not done) this" and similar ones. As Mariel writes, "I want you to know that self-blame is never the answer and never justified. No matter how you tried to protect and shield your loved one – you could not have prevented the outcome. You were limited in what you could do to prevent/stop the suicide from occurring."

"No suicide is ever the fault of another nor is it the fault of the victim either. Instead, see the fault as belonging to a range of other factors that create the potential for suicide, mental illness, society, environment, conditioning, bullying, sexual orientation, depression, financial losses, academic pressures and many more to name a few."

Reading this section made me think of an amazing statement I read many years ago by Ann Napier, at the time the chief editor of the British literary magazine *Cygnus*:

Seen from the eternal heart of the universe
all your choices are right choices
all your faltering are advantages
and you never did anything wrong

Another section that touched me deeply was the whole section on forgiveness. As one who has been running self-development workshops for close to thirty years, I believe that, with love, forgiveness is the most important spiritual/psychological dimension of life that exists. How many lives are stunted by the inability to forgive? Mariel gives the most powerful example of forgiveness I have ever come across in over eighty years of walking this planet, i.e. the story of the Polish lawyer who forgave the Nazis who gunned down his wife and five children in front of his eyes. At that moment, he explains, he had to decide between hatred and love, and he opted for the latter because, as a lawyer, he had too often seen what hatred can do to destroy people. He survived six years in Auschwitz in perfect health because he had decided to love every single person he met –

which he did.

I was personally deeply moved by the case story Mariel gives of Gregory, who had carefully planned his suicide, and fascinated by the amazing way she worked with him. In this respect, Mariel's sharing helps one to understand the numerous failures of modern psychiatry and a great deal of psychotherapy. One can easily imagine how a psychiatrist might have tried to handle Gregory's situation, completely missing the point. As a matter of fact, one cannot help wishing that Mariel's book were on the compulsory reading list of the students of all departments of psychiatry, so important it is to understand why psychiatry cannot heal many cases, as it is trying to approach situations with a tool that by definition cannot function.

The most powerful aspect of this book for me is that it is written entirely from the heart. Heart energy imbues its every page, yea, its every word. This is one of the reasons it is so easy to read, and so comforting, and also no doubt why we accept without questioning statements which written with a purely intellectual approach would leave one deeply skeptical.

And all through the book, you will find numerous very helpful exercises the reader can start practicing on the spot, like the most moving one on the preciousness of your human life.

I wish to conclude this forward by quoting the author who writes: "To those reading this book, I hope I have shone a light into the great unknown and given a glimpse of the eternal truth that fills this universe and embraces all living beings: that life is eternal. Release your fear of death and embrace the awesome possibilities that the afterlife awaits you. Remember it is love – not religion – which generates spiritual growth. Love is the creative source of the Universe. Indeed, divinity is love. It is through divinity that all things come into being and that all life has purpose.

Divinity created you and everything that ever existed – and proclaimed it good. Love is the powerful and constant source of energy that is available to you every moment of every second without fail."

Choose wisely how to live each and every moment...

"Trust that whatever you do to make a difference will add significantly to your evolving soul. And when it is your time to return home to the heart of God/creator you can do so without fear resulting in the most heavenly reunion. May you look at the process of death with renewed joy and hope in the knowing that beyond the veil of death a majestic and beautiful love awaits you."

Thank you, Mariel, for this infinitely precious gift you have made to the world.

Pierre Pradervand
Author, *The Gentle Art of Blessing*

Acknowledgments

To God my creator for your presence and guidance always in my life and for inspiring me to write this book. To my beloved Gallianna and all my higher Beings of love and light that have journeyed with me throughout my many incarnations. I am humbly grateful.

To the most incredible man that God placed before me, my husband Iggy. Thank you for believing in me when I lost belief in myself. Iggy, you have touched the very landscape of my soul throughout all eternity. Thank you for the journey together into the heart of oneness.

To my three beautiful creations, my son Keith, daughters Nicola and Shelley for continuing to teach me that life is a gift and to never give up on my wildest dreams. Keith, you taught me to listen without judgment and through you to love unconditionally. Shelley, your gentleness and soulful essence has brought love and wonderment always to my heart. A special welcome to our family Grant J. Nicola, you continue to teach me to view the playground of your world and see the incredible beauty in the simplest of all life forms. Without her unwavering help, technical support, patience and beautiful spirit this book would not be birthed. Thank you for the numerous hours over the years that you invested in my work. You are a gift to this world, a shining star glowing in the midnight sky. Thank you, I love you. Joanne, my daughter in-law, you are truly a blessing in my life and an amazing earth mother. Hannah, thank you for your love and support always.

To my grandchildren, Odhrán, Gemma and Elissa. Thank

you for keeping the magic and enchantment of life alive in all our encounters. To my grandchildren, yet to come, who are at present held in the womb of the Divine, know that I love you as I await your arrival upon sacred mother earth.

To my beloved soul brother of my heart Pierre Pradervand. Thank for your profound inspirational presence in my life. You are one of the most humble earth angels I am privileged to know. Thank you.

To my family Padraig, Anna, Gerry, Angela, Peter and my beloved Joseph, thank you for your timeless love and the many soul lessons we mastered together in this lifetime. Trust that we keep on growing and evolving in wholeness and sacredness. To Iggy's family for teaching me that sometimes silence is golden. I love and bless you all.

A special thank you to my precious friends whose love and support has always been a gift in my life especially: El, Anne, Patricia, Helen, Stephanie, Sinead and Mary O. To all those who have touched my life with your love: Mary & Martin, Anne & John, Martin Feeney. I am deeply humbled and may our journey together continue to be joyful and soulful.

To my faithful students who journeyed with me over the many years, you have been my greatest teachers, to each of you, thank you.

To John Hunt Publishing Company, may I extend my deepest gratitude for embracing the eclectic concepts within my book and recognizing its worthiness for publication.

Finally, I would like to extend my deepest gratitude to all my clients for allowing me to be the bridge between the two worlds and to witness the Divine in all things especially during times of a loved one's passing. I am forever grateful.

Personal Introduction

My personal journey has not been without many crosses to carry and many mountains to climb. All the challenges I once perceived as punishments from God, I now see as gifts. Since my own near-death experience in 1992, I have dedicated my life to exploring the mystery of life and death. Why did I survive three near-death experiences and live? I was born in the country in a rural part of Ireland. I was a tomboy and felt I was as good as my brothers, even better, when it came to hurling in the field, playing marbles and climbing trees. Sometimes I outstayed my welcome with them and they would disown me with an automatic expulsion. One day, however, I took matters into my own hands. While the boys ignored me I stole their football and climbed up a drainpipe onto a seventeen-foot flat roof. I was in heaven as I looked down at them searching everywhere for their ball. How powerful I felt shouting down at them and bouncing the ball to my heart's content. I knew they could never reach me. I continued to taunt them, skipping and bouncing the ball until I lost my footing and fell to the ground onto mass concrete. For some unknown reason I miraculously survived the fall with broken bones and a ribcage that will forever remain deformed. But I didn't die.

As teenagers our summers were spent in the local lake swimming and sailing. I was a strong swimmer and would swim in the deepest waters. On this occasion I swam from the largest diving board under the smaller one. As luck would have it I got caught under the diving board. I struggled to set myself free. I was running out of breath. Nobody noticed my struggle as I was underwater. I was paralyzed with fear, *"Is this the way I'm going to die, I don't want to die, I want to live."* As the last bit of air was leaving my lungs I felt someone lift me up and then push me out under the diving board. Coughing and choking and gasping for breath I looked round to say, *"Thank you,"* but alas, there was no one there; no one even noticed that I was drowning. Why was I saved again and who saved me? I questioned why some people die and why others live. This was the beginning of my quest into the meaning of life, what lies beyond the veil that divides the two worlds. Is this the veil that is pierced at death to allow the soul to travel outward into the world of Spirit? My parents were both Catholics but expressed an easy attitude towards religion. Sunday Mass was an absolute must in case we'd find ourselves in trouble Monday morning with the nuns as to who attended mass and who didn't. Saturday was a time to offload your sins to a priest hidden behind a mysterious curtain within a wooden box. My parents never imposed their religious beliefs or concepts upon me. The God I believed in was a loving all-encompassing God. The wrath of God and hell's damnation never appealed to me. While various religions offer many truths on the concept of death, I have come to the belief that no one religion has all the answers. I am happy to say that I am one of the most naturally skeptical people you'll ever meet and I am addicted to research. My faith in God has always been unshakable, but unless I've seen, touched, felt and experienced the details about how the whole creation of His works, I take absolutely nothing for granted and keep digging for answers. Because of my years of intense research and studies in this area of life and afterlife I have learned to embrace all religious deities, be it God, Allah, Buddha, Krishna, Great White Spirit. I believe it's the one source of universal consciousness that over lights each of us throughout life.

My schooldays were very confusing and made more so by the fact that I attended a convent school for my education. On one hand I had the nuns telling me of a loving God presence if I was good, but if I was bad then a wicked devil armed with a two-pronged pitchfork was ready to cast me into the roaring fires of hell. Even as a young girl if things didn't make sense to me I would challenge and explore them relentlessly until they did. Oftentimes I was punished for my curiosity and left facing a blank wall behind the blackboard until religious class was over. Then along came my first confession, going into a wooden box and exposing my sins to a priest I couldn't even see. I had my sins learned off by heart, giving cheek to my mother, not doing what I was told, not brushing my teeth and calling names to my brothers and sisters. The priest told me how sorry I should be and what God wanted me to do to atone for my sins. Almost like a judge in court I was handed down my sentence. I had to say one *Our Father* and ten *Hail Marys* and promise never to offend again. Did I think my behavior was worthy of such a sentence? Of course not. Neither did it make sense to me that the God who created and loved me with all his heart could also be so cruel and hateful.

Back then if you ate meat on Friday you would be doomed to the fires of hell for all eternity (now it is acceptable to eat meat on Fridays). I wonder what happened to those unfortunate souls who thought they were going to hell because they ate meat on Friday. I remember back how cruel and unjust the Catholic teachings were as we honor those gone before us who were the beneficiaries of this heaven-hell dichotomy. My mother was a very enlightened woman and way before her time. It was in the early sixties, when she had seven children, that she decided to take the birth control pill. At that time in Ireland the missions came to your parish and everyone was obliged to go to confession. My poor mother went into the confessional box and confessed to the priest that she was on the contraceptive pill. What happened next she never forgot. He jumped out of his confessional box, opened the door where she knelt and pulled her out in front of the whole church. He shouted at her saying she was a fornicating woman and that her role was to bring as many children into the world equal to the amount of stars in the sky. While she was running with shame down the aisle he continued to roar after her with his last rant echoing, "go home and please your husband." Needless to say my mother never attended the missions again and thereafter went to the local monastery to an old monk who treated her with dignity and respect, who also apologized for the wrongdoings of the accusing priest.

As I got older the whole process of confession always seemed illogical to me; I didn't believe I needed an intermediary between my God and me. The God I connected with was an all-encompassing one who never judges or punishes anyone. While I would never disrespect my Catholic upbringing or any other religion for that matter, whether or not I agree with each and every detail of a religion it boils down to the same integral message: love God, do random acts of kindness and leave this earth a better place because you were part of it. I needed to educate myself until I found a belief system that resonated with me in every facet of my life and secure enough information to back it up. My true quest into life, death and rebirth became the embryonic fluid that coursed through my soul. I devoured many spiritual and religious books. I travelled far and wide learning about energy, vibration, frequency, chakras, soul keys, visited sacred sites while encountering many teachers along my path who endorsed my view on life and its spiritual significance. I promised myself not to be too hasty to accept or reject any ideology and to keep searching for the ultimate truth that death is not an end, but a beginning into another realm of consciousness. The eternal journey of the soul will be discussed throughout this book giving rise to an afterlife through reincarnation, near-death experiences, out-of-body experiences, past life regression and evidential documentation lifting the veil of ignorance to the ultimate truth – life does not end at physical death, it continues onwards.

> *Do not mourn because the caterpillar has become a beauteous butterfly. Do not weep because the cage has been opened and the bird has been set free. Rejoice and know that the enfranchised soul has found liberty and that, if you would but unfold the powers that the Great Spirit has given you, you could understand the plan of death and realize that death is but a stepping stone, a door through which you enter into the larger freedom of the realms of Spirit.*
> **Silver Birch**

Part 1: Fear of Death

Many of us avoid the idea of facing our mortality; we chase away all thoughts of death and dying in the hope it will never come to our door. This is primarily due to our fear around death, the fear of the unknown. I am blessed to work with many people who are nearing their end of life's journey. Some are old and are waiting in the departure lounge for death to call them. Others are terminally ill and feel that life is unfair and unjust. Others are young and regret the loss of time that they will never have. There are no answers as to why some die young and why others live within an imprisoned body where the mind has fallen asleep. As a spirit midwife *(a person who assists the dying in a handover process into the world of spirit)* I am invited by the family to sit at the bedside of the dying while using various energy modalities to assist the patient to cross over feeling loved and without fear. Afterwards I work with the bereaved families to help them continue to feel the presence of their loved one by using practical methods of afterlife communication which will be discussed later in this book.

Scientific Name for Fear of Death

Thanatophobia is the scientific name given to the fear of dying and death. Overcoming the fear of death requires a belief beyond doubt that a heavenly and most beautiful place awaits you in an afterlife. We need to feel safe within our deaths, and to feel that safety, we must turn the *"unknown"* into a known. Whether you are religious or not rituals are important for creating a sense of meaning in life. They also give continuity to our very existence.

Death is inevitable, and regardless of whatever belief system you were born into the soul has its own timing for its coming and its going. Embracing our mortality means we embrace our deaths and take time to live our lives in a positive healthy way. There is more to life than what we see, feel and hear during our waking consciousness. Imagine never having to worry about death again because we know that when we die, we are merely shedding the physical body and returning to a higher plane of consciousness. Many doctors and scientists mentioned have endorsed the concept of life beyond physical death by adding their names and credentials in support of an afterlife. It is my deepest wish to bring hope and comfort to those bereaved by the loss of a loved one, bringing the reader on a journey of self-discovery, with an awakening desire to discover the existence of life beyond the veil of death.

Death is our wedding with Eternity.
Rumi

Spiritual Immortality

It is natural to fear what we cannot see, and since death is a certainty, we react to it with fear. The biblical definition: physical death is the separation of the soul from God: *"Then the Dust will Return to the Earth as it was, and the Spirit will return to God who gave it"* (Ecclesiastes 12:7). A medical dictionary defines death as the cessation of all vital functions of the body, including the heartbeat, brain activity, brain stem and breathing. Both definitions are in stark contrast to each other. One offers hope of a return to a Godhead while the other offers nothing. In *Conversations with God* Neale Donald Walsch asked God, *"Why are we here upon this earth? Who are we? What is our purpose here?"* God replied, *"That each and every one of us is an Individuated Aspect of Divinity, travelling on a journey through the endless cycle of life, so that we may know and experience ourselves as whom we really are at any time during that cycle."* On evaluation of this statement I pose the question, *"Who are we really?"* I believe we are facets of that divinity made in the image of a creator God. I believe we are divine beings occupying a human body, having a human experience. At our core is a spark of divinity of perfect love which needs to be awakened. We don't go to heaven, we grow to heaven. The spiritual growth we have attained in this lifetime is the spiritual condition we take with us after death. When we die, we simply step into the spiritual condition we have cultivated throughout our lives. Near-death experiences reveal heaven to be about deeds not creeds. Everyone, religious or not, believing in God or not, transitions to the spirit world as part of the natural process of life. The more we live in love the closer we come to God. This is because love is God, and this love is the connection, the glue that holds people together. Love holds everything in the universe together. Love is the language that speaks within the heart; it is the center of the universe. Love is the universal key that opens the gateway to our immortality.

The Journey of the Soul

What if you slept and what if in your sleep, you dreamed and what if in your dream, you went to heaven and there plucked a strange and beautiful flower, and what if, when you woke, you had the flower in your hand. Ah, what then.
Samuel T. Coleridge

Julie Soskin, in her book *The Wind of Change* (Barton House, 1990), talks of the soul *"being our unique energy, each with its own light."* *Webster's Dictionary* defines the soul as *"an entity without material reality, regarded as the spiritual part of a person."* Larry Dossey defines the soul *"as some aspect of the psyche that is not subject to the limitations of space and time, which may precede birth and survives death."* The concept of the soul being immortal is not a new style of thinking. The scriptures talk of eternal life, referring to the immortality of the soul, not the physical body. As early as the 4th century BCE Pythagoras wrote of the soul being separate from the body and in death would be reunited with God. In Eastern culture death is seen as a brief stopping point on an endless soul journey whereby you could be a pauper in one lifetime or a prince in another. Thus adding to the concept of the soul reincarnating time and time again until it has mastered the life lessons which the soul agreed to achieve.

What is Soul? It is the Essence of who you truly are

The soul is a candle that will burn away the darkness. Only the glorious duties of love we will have. My soul is a candle that burned away the veil. Only the glorious duties of light I now have.
St. John of the Cross

Plato the Greek philosopher is considered to be the first to write on the definition of the soul. He defined the soul as *"a sensation as a communication between soul and body."* According to Plato the body was *"the medium for the soul."* Aristotle regarded the soul *"as the sum of the vital principles as being to the body what vision is to the eye."* The soul was to him the true being in the body. While the definition of soul has varied down through the ages, the one prevailing commonality throughout is that it is the soul that defines us not the body.

I believe the body is the temple of the soul and as my work continues to expand more specifically in the area of light body healing and soul retrieval, I have found that no matter how much you may identify with your body – your body is not you. Remember you are eternal and the soul is that spiritual part of you that never dies. Your physical body has its term of contract. It only lasts a lifetime; just like a pair of old shoes you have outworn, you step out of them to walk again in a brand-new pair. *(This will be discussed later in the section on reincarnation.)* The physical body is the vehicle that houses your soul while having its earth experience. The soul holds the consciousness of who you truly are. The soul carries within it the memories and experiences of all your lifetimes. The soul contains the divine essence of Creator/God which is within you and me and every single human on this planet. It is this Divine essence that gives us access to eternal life.

In other words our bodies are simply empty vessels without the existence of the soul. Everything has a soul. An animal has a soul. A tree, a flower has a soul. A rock has a soul. Everything in the universe has a soul. Your soul holds the experience and the emotions of all of the choices you have made in this lifetime and every other incarnation of your soul evolution. Millions of people believe in the spiritual world. This faith may be expressed through a religion or other belief system. I believe in the Divine (Creator or Source) and as the creator of the universe the Divine embraces all religions and belief systems encompassing Saints, Buddhas, Angels, Ascended Masters, which are all part of the divine creation. As human beings we live in the physical world where we uphold and respect the laws of our country. Whether we consciously know or understand it, our souls are governed by spiritual laws that over light the universe. Our physical life is inseparable from our spiritual life and vice versa. This is becoming increasingly evident as more and more people are searching consciously for soul illumination to help them fulfill their spiritual quest. Everything and everyone has a spiritual life and physical life. A soul in the universe has a spiritual existence, it has a spiritual life. When a soul reincarnates as a human being, it takes on a physical body. Spiritual life and physical life are distinct from each other yet they are entwined as they serve each other. When the life's mission upon earth is complete the silver cord disengages from the physical body and the soul moves outwards back to the Creator/Source.

When my mother was dying, I found it a most humbling experience to be at her bedside during her final days. Coming from a large family, we were equally blessed that we were able to care for her in her own home surrounded by her loved ones. As a family we held vigil around her bedside, with each member of the family spending quality time with her. Living in the country in rural Ireland has its blessings especially when someone is about to return home. The sense of belonging and being part of an extended country family was no different for my mother. Neighbors came to bid their final farewell to a generous, dignified and well-liked lady. While cups of tea with little shots of whiskey were drunk stories of old and memories of the past filtered through the air as we were comforted in our wait for her time to come.

At approximately 8:30am the morning of her passing, the palliative care nurse called us rather suddenly, saying there was a notable change in my mother. As we gathered around her bed, I could see the most amazing mist of golden light around her. I could visibly see that her soul was rising up from her body and beginning to move above her. I would describe this vision as a photocopy of her body but a lighter version of it. At that moment I felt humbled to become the silent witness in my own mother's transitioning process. I gently whispered to my younger sister Angela and asked her, "Can you see what's happening?" She answered, "See what?" A feeling of infinite peace enveloped each of us as we waited for my mother's time to come. Hours went by and she didn't seem to be going anywhere. I asked for private time with her to check in spiritually to see what was holding her back. Through communication with my angels and guides I was shown other lifetimes where she had died in horrific circumstances. The imprints of these traumas were still held within her light body.

After receiving permission from her soul I began working on releasing the trauma of these deaths. Upon completion I was guided to hold her hands and take her on the journey home through visualization. This was a most precious and sacred exchange between our two souls as I was spiritually handing her over through the veil into the next life. I requested a bridge of light to be placed before her as I knew there was no way she would enter any tunnel because of her mortal fears. Not only did I see a golden bridge, but I saw Mother Mary standing midway on the pathway. (My mother had a huge devotion to Mother Mary all her life.) Spiritually I was allowed to walk with her towards Mother Mary, then I was told it was time to place her hand within Mother Mary's and say farewell. This was a heartbreaking moment as I held and kissed her and reassured her all was well. She walked with Mother Mary, and as she looked back I told her, *"It's okay to go now."* She smiled and walked towards a magnificent light. Before the light disappeared from my psychic vision I was shown clearly my father waiting on the right side of the bridge with my young brother Joseph waiting to the left. Joseph was waving and beckoning her to move forward towards him. Both were there waiting to meet her and take her home. Moments before she took her final breath she rose up from her bed, leaned forward with her eyes transfixed in the corner of the room. As she held that gaze she smiled at something, then laid back in her bed and moments later exhaled her final breath. Without doubt I know it was my father and brother Joseph who came to take her hand and lead her home.

The Silver Cord

Dr. Dianne Morrissey spoke after her near-death experience stating, *"I saw a long silver cord coming out of my spirit body, right through the cheese cloth-like fabric I was wearing. The cord extended down and out in front of me, and as I turned around, I saw that the silver cord draped around and behind me, like an umbilical cord. The cord was about an inch wide and sparkled like Christmas tree tinsel."*

In Dr. PMH Atwater's book *Beyond the Light* the near-death

account of Alice Morrison Mays is given. Alice described her return to her physical body from a near-death experience. She remembers entering her physical body through the silver cord: *"Almost instantly I felt reentry into my body through the silver cord at the top of my head. As soon as I entered, I heard someone near me say, 'Oh, we've got her back.'"* Those who endorse near-death experiences have felt the pull of the silver cord when it is stretched near its limit. They often describe the experience as being instantly retracted to their physical body – like stretching a rubber band to its limit and then releasing it back on itself.

The silver cord keeps the soul connected to the body throughout its lifetime on earth and is only broken at the moment of physical death. The silver cord has been mentioned in many of the world's religions including the biblical reference in Ecclesiastes 12:6-7, *"Before the silver cord is snapped and the soul returns to the God who gave it."* The silver cord is limitless and can stretch beyond the earth's plane into the realm of spirit during our dream or sleep state. The cord nourishes the soul with the life force of God/Creator and only disengages from the physical body when the earth's journey is complete. During the dying process as the soul leaves the physical body the silver cord becomes thinner as it is stretched to its limit and eventually snaps. When this happens it is not possible for the soul to reenter the body; this stage is known as the point of no return.

My Vision of Witnessing the Silver Cord: Yvette my Friend

During writing this book three of my close friends made their transition home. I treasure all of them equally but one in particular touched my soul very deeply. Her name was Yvette, she loved life, her passion was dancing and she choreographed many a sequence for both stage and television performances. When she was diagnosed with cancer she accepted her fate with courage and dignity. Not once did she utter, *"Why me?"* Instead she kept her spirits high by listening to meditations, doing affirmations, and reading spiritual books. During this time she still managed to hold down her full-time job as a dance master and never said a word to anyone. She was a private lady and one can only imagine how I felt when she confided her trust in me about her prognosis. Yvette was a soul seeker and a highly evolved one at that. She showed great admiration for my work while taking refuge in the knowledge that this was the biggest soul lesson she needed to master.

After one of our healing sessions Yvette asked if I could be with her when her time to transition came. I told her it was a promise I could not make as the soul decides its time for going and it also decides who (if anyone) is to be present as they take their last breath. However, I did say, "If it was divinely orchestrated, I would be humbled to share in your final journey and pass you through the veil into the world of spirit." This made her very happy and with a cheeky grin on her face said, *"Oh you'll be there."* When the time came for Yvette to enter the hospice there was no fuss, no dramas, no procrastination, just a gentle surrender to the inevitable. When I knew her time to exit was drawing close, I worked on her energy bodies and began recoiling her chakra systems. This shamanic practice makes it easier for the soul to rise from the body without being held back by the limitations of the physical body. I could see her soul hovering above her physical body for hours before the most incredible phenomenon occurred.

Minutes before Yvette passed into the world of spirit – I was blessed with the most miraculous and profound experience I could ever imagine. I will cherish it till the day I physically die. While I held vigil around her body my eyes were drawn to the upper part of her body. Time stood still as I absorbed the vision before me. For the first and only time in my life, I could visibly see the silver cord. It was a delicate luminescent silvery thread that was pulling away from beneath her breastbone. During this time tiny particles of golden mist continued spiraling around her head. This radiance had its own life force. I could see the silver cord in all its majesty and mystery moving upwards to the top left side of her head. Suddenly, the cord was consumed within the golden mist. For one brief moment in time – I witnessed the point of no return – the silver cord vanished into nothingness as Yvette passed through the veil into the world of spirit. All that was left was a golden mist that formed a halo effect around her beautiful head. Then the reality of what happened began to sink in. Yvette's parting can only be described as a true Epiphany; as a surge of the most hallowed awe caressed the very core of my soul. There are no words on earth to describe the heavenly experience that I was privileged to witness. Nothing will ever compare to that rarest moment where life ends and the journey begins.

How could the soul not take flight, when from the glorious Presence a soft call flows sweet as honey, comes right up to her and whispers, "Rise up now, come away."
Rumi

Where is the Soul Located?

Throughout the ages the soul has been the subject of much discussion and argument not only by its definition but also as to where it resides in the human body. Research shows that there is no true consensus on where the soul is in location. Philosophers, psychologists and scientists, such as Socrates, Plato, Aristotle, Swedenborg and Descartes, all believed the soul's existence was the most divine part of the human psyche. However, its precise location varied in that some believed it resided in the heart while others believed it was in the head. Personally, I believe the soul is the ultimate life force that animates the body. It is everywhere while it spreads its consciousness over the entire body. The most comprehensive explanation of where the soul resides has come direct from my spiritual guide Gallianna.

The soul resides nowhere in the body, for it is immaterial, yet is resides everywhere. The soul drives the mind, the will and the emotions. Thus it lives within the mind, urging the thoughts to the Highest Will for its wisest good. It lives in the heart, driving man towards Good deeds and true love, unconditional, leading the emotions. And it resides still yet in the brain, guiding the actions and thoughts, embracing the memories and calming the fears, yet it is a whisper and a consoling gentleness. Thus it is oftentimes drowned by the loud voice of man's own reasoning, it is a persuading mother, thus it is oftentimes ignored by the petulance of the child acting out. Yet even more so, it is a warmth and a knowing in the heart, which can be so readily chilled by man's own stubborn readiness to disallow compassion to spoil its plan. Thus all of the answers are right. But none of them are enough to know all that the soul really is, or where she lies. She is in all of you.

Gallianna, Heaven's Ambassador

Meditation is a natural way that helps open up the spiritual channels within the body. With practice a bridge of light is activated to your higher consciousness/God which brings you into alignment with your soul's purpose on earth. In time, you will see images of the spiritual world and other dimensions beyond the comprehension of your physical sight. For those whose spiritual channels are dormant or asleep, the soul remains invisible. Your soul possesses incredible wisdom accumulated from many experiences and memories of other lifetimes. Your soul holds the key to unlocking the library of infinite lives lived. Your soul may travel when you are asleep to learn from your spiritual guides and teachers in the inner realms. (The concept of out-of-body experience will be discussed in a later chapter.) When you are spiritually awake and your spiritual channels are open, you can communicate with your soul. You will be fascinated at how much knowledge and wisdom your soul knows.

Soul Lessons: Important challenges to help you Evolve

Before you reincarnate there are certain lessons the soul agrees to undertake in order to redress any imbalances that may have been created in previous lifetimes. For example, your soul may choose to be born into a dysfunctional family. This dysfunction could range from alcohol/drug abuse and violent behaviors where total disrespect for humankind is ignored. Each member of such a family have lessons yet to learn. If these lessons are not mastered through time, the family will find themselves in a vicious cycle of repeated patterns lifetime after lifetime. However, if a member of the same dysfunctional family in their next incarnation chooses to be born into a peaceful and harmonious environment this would break the vicious cycle of abuse. The soul now chooses to learn to grow soulfully within a loving family unit, resulting in tremendous advancement for that particular soul. When you have mastered the life lessons that your soul agreed, be it loss, compassion, love, illness, fear, poverty or trauma, you will finally reach a stage of spiritual enlightenment. What this expression means is that a person who has lived many lifetimes finally has advanced to a state of divine perfection. Achieving this state means the soul no longer needs to reincarnate in a human body as it is fully conscious, and its divine essence is reabsorbed back into the light of the creator.

What are Spiritual Blockages?

I believe that spiritual blockages are the result of mistakes made in previous lifetimes or your present life. There is a golden rule which states, *"Do unto others as you would have them do unto you"* (Matthew 7:12): be mindful what you give out to the world. For example, parents who respect and love their own parents will generally have children who will love and respect them. On the other hand, people who do not treat their parents with love and respect will receive similar treatment from their own children. Generally speaking if you show love to others, you will receive love in return. For a moment reflect on your own life and the lives of your loved ones and friends. Do any of them repeat the same mistakes over and over again in their personal lives, their careers, their family or personal relationships? Why do they suffer from chronic health problems? Why are they stuck in the same patterns of behavior? Why do some have such bad luck? The answer is Karma. The Bible says, *"Whatsoever a man soweth, that shall he also reap"* (Galatians 6:7), which describes Karma simply but perfectly. Life is a precious gift and what you do with that life is about the choices you make and how you honor and respect all life forms. Your life is like a balance sheet with the sum total of good deeds versus bad deeds. With good deeds you earn grace and virtue, with bad deeds you earn Karma. Begin today by reflecting on your mistakes and what is not working for you. When you are willing to acknowledge the divinity in others you are allowing them to continue with their Karma without you being a participant in their karmic journey. If you are unwilling or unable to forgive someone with whom you are in crisis, know you are stunting your own soul growth. Always remember when you apply unconditional love and forgiveness to a situation, Karma is healed.

Give yourself time to reflect on the following statements:

- Is there someone you need to forgive today?
- Is there someone you need to say I am sorry – please forgive me?
- Is there someone who needs your love and attention today?
- Is there someone you continue to hold judgments against?
- Is there someone who needs your hand of friendship today?
- Is there someone you hurt badly years ago?

If you answer "yes" to any or all of the above begin now by clearing your karmic debt and right the wrong of your actions. In doing so you will receive many blessings in every aspect of your life with good virtue being recorded in your book of life.

Exercise to awaken your Soul

To evolve the soul fully one must master the energies of love, compassion, forgiveness, trust, gratitude, faith, grace and humbleness. A healthy attitude rejoices the soul and the art of forgiveness empowers it. Develop a sacred communication with your soul as a doorway to your God/Self by doing the following exercise.

As you begin to answer take a few deep breaths and listen with that part of you that is awake enough now to hear the answers.

- Make a list of belief systems that limit your growth, for example: I'm not good enough, I'm too old, I always fail, good things only happen to other people, all people are bad etc.
- Make another list of what you know, in the depths of your heart, to be true about yourself.
- Make a list of judgments you still hold about yourself.
- Make a list of judgments you hold about others.
- Make a list of patterns/mistakes you keep repeating.

Always remember the hardest lessons being presented to you are not always the easiest ones to master. Often those presenting you with the greatest challenges are usually your greatest teachers upon mother earth.

My First Experience of Seeing a Soul

In my personal work I perceive the soul as having its own individual blueprint, just like the snowflake where no two flakes are the same. The first time I saw a soul was during a healing session with Frankie, a 48-year-old man. As he stepped into my healing room, I could clearly see his soul was looming outside his body in the form of a mirror image of himself only transparent. During the healing session I was shown the exact time his soul exited his body. He was a seven-year-old boy in the care of his grandfather when he was brutally raped by him. At that point his soul vacated his body in order to feel no pain from the traumatic experience. His soul remained disengaged from his body from that time until he came to me for light body healing. Throughout the healing his soul continued to come in and out of his body. Eventually, his soul agreed to be reunited with his body through a soul retrieval process. As an incredible light force encapsulated his body he walked out the door feeling powerful, in charge of his life and happier than he had felt for years. Frankie returned for a few more sessions; with each time his appearance was changing, he was fresher, younger and most of all he had found a zest for life. He finally met someone with whom he intended to share his life with without the traumas of the past coming back to haunt him.

Witness to real life Karma presenting itself from a Previous Life

Many years ago I travelled to Mount Shasta, California to attend a spiritual retreat. Mount Shasta is a very special place. It represents much more than a mere mountain as it is one of the most sacred places on the earth. Mount Shasta is a mystical power source for this earth and is considered as the embodiment of the great central sun. I attended a series of workshops by Dr. Zhi Gang Sha on *Soul Mind Body Medicine*. Dr. Sha was an empowering teacher and wonderful healer with a valuable message for us as participants. His teachings taught us the power of the soul to influence and transform all life. His most influential teaching was heal the soul first, then healing of the mind and body will follow.

I was transfixed by the power of his words and the resonance they held for me. I had a sense of knowing and being familiar with his spoken words. During one of his talks Dr. Sha put forward the theory that the Law of Karma is exact. It is a natural law just like gravity is a natural law. If in a previous lifetime your actions harmed others, you may decide to incarnate in your next lifetime to undo the wrongs you perpetrated upon others. A wonderful example of this was magnified when a young American girl in her late twenties stepped onto the stage. She related her life story of having chronic neck and back pain since she was a child. Her symptoms were so severe that no medication could relieve her constant pain. As a last resort she underwent serious spinal surgery. A mesh cage was placed inside her body running from the top of her neck down her spine. This was to help her walk without falling over. She was suicidal and her pain was unbearable. Dr. Sha had the ability to look within her Akashic records or book of life.

Her story unraveled: in a previous lifetime she was a cruel executioner and took pleasure in seeing others hang by the neck. She showed no mercy and delighted in the pain she inflicted upon them *(it's important to point out she occupied a male body in that incarnation)*. The imprints of past behavior were presenting itself in this lifetime for healing. Her soul called forth the experiences and provided her with the opportunity to rebalance her karmic debt. It all made sense to her; she always knew she was stuck in some prison of self but could not escape, no matter how hard she tried. With her permission Dr. Sha cleared her light body and removed the cords that held her imprisoned within her own body. She had work to do but she was ready to bring harmony and balance back into her life by doing selfless acts of kindness and forgiving herself for the injustices she previously caused. When she stepped off the stage she looked utterly transformed, she was smiling, the pain had left her face. She looked younger as she descended the steps effortlessly and easily in comparison to her struggle to mount the steps earlier to go onstage. Her karmic cycle of persecution was finally healed through forgiveness and unconditional love. When I returned to Ireland I was most mindful of how I interacted and treated others. I tried to uphold a non-judgmental presence in all situations where I was neither judge nor jury. I became more silent about my assumptions of others and only contributed to conversations that were positive and coming from a loving space within my heart. This practice of non-judgment has become my holy grail and one that continues to serve me gracefully on my soul journey.

The Sweetness of the Soul

Archangel Raziel explains the meaning of the Soul in our Lives.

The soul believes the common truth, that we are conscious beings capable of having deep understanding in a moment in time of the reality of the soul. This is because the capacity of the soul is an all-encompassing version of self, borne out of the four states of body form. It is an ever evolving, translucent, look at the human's interaction with its environment and the air it breathes. It is lodged in a place of higher power and is linked to galaxies and to the underlying truth that the mighty has done great things for me and always will. It is the part of us that allows the capacity of the human entity to float free from any restrictions on this earth. It is the part of us that does not conform to that which is not the truth as we perceive it. A soul will use its consciousness to evolve continuously. It does not have a yard stick that it expects us to perform to. It weaves many varied paths to give us each and every experience that the soul needs to reach an understanding of its multifaceted self. It knows when it is happy. It knows when the vibration it is receiving from the universe matches the energy that it emits in response to the stimuli it has been exposed to. It will hold honor and order in the court of your life to move you to the best experiential experience possible for you in your human form as a high vibrational being.

It will strive to align your soul to be a reflection of your creator in your highest glory. It is your best barometer of idealism for you and when aligned the human connection to the soul will be felt through oneness with all beings and entities which mingle with you. You will express these great moments of Euphoria and Joy.

Natalie Glasson

Scientific Evidence Supporting Near-Death Experiences and Afterlife

Reincarnation, Past Life Regression, Near-Death Experiences, Out-of-Body Experiences, Deathbed Visions, After Death Communication, Visitations.

I have always wondered and questioned the meaning of life, death and the word *immortality*. Throughout this chapter I will provide indisputable evidence which comes from volumes of research and evidential proof from doctors, scientists, physicists, psychologists, professors and many more – who without their own personal brush with another reality did not believe nor endorse the concept that life continues beyond physical death. Or that the human soul is reincarnated on earth time and time again until it reaches perfection. Extraordinary accounts of what takes place when we die are featured throughout. It is my greatest wish that you the reader will be liberated from the prison of your fears surrounding death, and the evidence presented will transform the way you think of what lies ahead.

Reincarnation

Is defined in the *Oxford Dictionary*: *"A Rebirth of a Soul in a new Body."* I believe deeply in reincarnation and the journey of the soul. This comes from personal experiences and my work with clients over many years. You may not believe in the concept of reincarnation and that is perfectly okay. I'm not here to impose my personal beliefs on anyone. I honor and respect everyone's beliefs. But I am convinced that when we die, the soul goes back to Source, and after a period of learning will return again to begin another lifetime if the soul lessons were not mastered in the previous one. Throughout many years of experiences and extensive research, one of the most compelling discoveries was that most of the world's great religions, including Christianity until it was restructured by Pope Constantine in the 6th century, accepted the truth of reincarnation and the evolving cycle of the soul from one lifetime to another. It was not until the Second Council of Constantinople in 553 CE that reincarnation was declared a heresy and any mention of it was removed from all public texts. Constantine did not like the idea of people getting multiple chances to return to redress any wrongs they may have done, because that would mean people did not need the Church to offer its people pardon for the salvation of their souls.

However, a few references to reincarnation managed to remain intact after his reign. The following references are from the revised standard version of the Bible that was written after Pope Constantine. For example, the 9th chapter of John tells the story of a man who was born blind. The disciples asked Jesus, *"Master who did sin, this man, or his parents, that he was born blind?"* The disciples acknowledged the possibility that being born blind might be this man's punishment for sins he committed. But because he was born blind, when did he get time to sin unless it was from a previous life. Another reference to reincarnation comes from Matthew (11:13-15). Jesus was talking to Peter, James and John and said, *"Elijah does come, and he is to restore all things, but I tell you that Elijah has already come."* This is the clearest biblical reference endorsing reincarnation that John the Baptist is Elijah who has already come. In the Aramaic Gospel of the Nazarenes the idea of reincarnation is a reality. Here Jesus speaks of the true resurrection, *"Just as all beings come into the world from the invisible realms, so will they all return to the invisible;*

and they will continue to come again in this way until they are purified. Those who return shall receive a new body and that which they have sown in one life shall they reap in another." (Nazarenes/Gospel of Holy Twelve 94:2-6) The ultimate purpose of reincarnation is for the overall evolution of the soul which may take many lifetimes before it advances to the higher level of existence and becomes one with God/Creator.

There are many people who have dedicated their lives in researching the phenomenon of life beyond death and I will mention a few here. Reincarnation was finally scientifically proven through the outstanding research into the subject by scientist Ian Stevenson. In 1958, Professor Stevenson submitted a paper on "Proof of Life after Death" through claims made by those who remembered previous incarnations. He dedicated his life to finding and verifying cases to prove that reincarnation is fact. For years he travelled all over the world to conquer the uncharted territory of reincarnation in the name of medical science. He collected more than 2,500 reports of cases on reincarnation. His relentless work with hundreds of children having vivid recall of past lives laid the foundation for future research of this kind. Seventy of these case studies he describes in great detail in his book entitled *Reincarnation and Biology*. On June 11th, 1992 at Princeton University Dr. Stevenson presented a paper entitled "Birthmarks and Birth Defects Corresponding to Wounds on Deceased Persons," providing scientific evidence suggestive of reincarnation which was published in the *Journal of Scientific Exploration*. These results support reincarnation in NDE research findings as well. Reincarnation has been called by some to be the greatest unknown scientific discovery. The last chapter of Professor Stevenson's book *20 Cases Suggestive of Reincarnation* (1967) provides rigorous scientific reasoning to show how reincarnation is the only viable explanation that fits the facts of his study. He considers every possible alternative explanation for his twenty cases of young children who were spontaneously able to describe a previous lifetime as soon as they learned to talk. Supported by overwhelming evidence the children's stories about their past lives invariably confirm that reincarnation is a reality for us all. His work was the start of a whole new modern-day approach to research into reincarnation. In 2007, Professor Stevenson returned home to spirit, leaving humanity a legacy of scientific proof on reincarnation rather than mere speculations gleaned from the philosophers of old.

The Influence of Reincarnation on my Personal Life

Because of my unwavering belief in the evolving journey of my soul I understand the consequences that reincarnation and Karma have regarding my present lifetime. How I think and behave around people is a choice I make. The following is a list of beliefs that have enriched my life for the better.

- I am no longer afraid of death, as I understand that my soul is eternal and never dies.
- When I lose someone I love, although I experience sadness, I know they continue to live on in another plane of existence and that communication still exists on a spiritual level.
- I respect all of humanity, regardless of color, skin, race, creed, sexual orientation.
- I never look down on another because they are disabled, poor, speak differently or look differently, because through them I am being taught a valuable life lesson.
- I see events and tragic circumstance as important lessons for me to grow and master.
- I see myself as the architect of my life and I am responsible for everything that happens to me.
- I know that if I abuse love, one day I will be the one treated unlovingly.
- I see each day as a gift from God. Therefore I am grateful

for each day I am given, to embrace love in order to grow and evolve spiritually.

I am happy my years of research into the life we lead as souls may assist survivors in recognizing death only exchanges one reality for another in the long continuum of existence.
Michael Newton, Master Regression Therapist

Personal Past Life Regression – Personal Evidence that I lived before

Past life regression provides major evidence in support of reincarnation. Past life regression simply involves a person under hypnosis going back through their childhood to an earlier time. In many cases the person begins talking about his or her life or lives before the present lifetime, about their previous death and about the time between lives including the planning of the present lifetime.

As I previously stated I am a natural skeptic and must see, feel, touch and know before I believe. My skepticism was truly put to the test when I offered myself as a human guinea pig to a past life regression session. This lady was my friend and renowned in her field in regression therapy using past life recall to heal present-day fears and phobias. She had her work cut out for her. Hypnotize me – not a chance – I even slept with one eye open. However, within minutes of counting down I was in another place, during another time in history. I was in France, standing in front of a water fountain, my hands tied with a rope behind my back. I was wearing what appeared to be a vintage lace dress, bare feet, I had a very pale complexion with long blonde hair. As I viewed my surroundings I saw people crying, while children ran innocently around those assembled. Suddenly the air became still with what I can only describe and remember as a massive drum roll. In that moment, two soldiers grabbed me and forced my face down into the fountain. I struggled underwater as I gasped for air. The next thing I felt was a pair of hands tightening around my neck making sure to squeeze the last breath from me. I remember leaving my body and floating out of it, a feeling of peace enveloping me as I looked back at my lifeless body being dragged from the fountain and thrown onto a cart. Next thing I remember was the sound of my friend's voice counting down and bringing me back to conscious awareness.

What the hell just happened there, I shouted. She told me I had gone back to a previous lifetime in France, and while I was under spoke in French with a French accent. This nugget of wisdom was manna from heaven for me as I could totally relate to the findings. While at school I absolutely loved French and loved to embellish the French accent. I often hopped onstage and would sing every French song I ever knew, and if I ran out of songs would make up my own and blast them out to the rhythm of any Abba tune. The most profound commonality in all of this was the fact that for years I suffered with hoarseness and sore throats. Sometimes my throat would be red raw and bleed for no apparent reason. This continued well into my adulthood, until I had a tonsillectomy at the age of 24 years. This elevated my symptoms at a physical level. Only to discover that it would be years later that the real healing would begin through past life healing. Months later I had another past life regression and went back to the same lifetime in France, but this time the therapist asked me, *"What age are you now?"* In my best French accent I said 24. This was ironic as it tied in with my drowning at the fountain in France aged 24, and my present-life tonsillectomy at the age of 24.

Over the years I continued to allow myself to be a subject in many past life regression sessions. This of course was to feed my insatiable quest for knowledge and to test my skepticism further. It unfolded I had many lifetimes in France, where I had the ability to view my death on numerous occasions. Not only was I drowned in a fountain in Southern France, but two other past lives involved me being burnt at the stake. In those days, I was born with natural gifts and did not conform or bend to the behest of society. I was skilled in divination and possessed psychic powers including healing gifts. I was heralded as a witch and burned at the stake. One of the most significant regression sessions occurred when I found myself in Egypt. I was a high priestess in the Temple of Alexandria. (Alexandria was once known as the place of wisdom and science.) My hair was black; I wore a cream flowing dress with gold embellishments on cords across my bust area. My sandals were gold and my skin was dark. My eyes looked like two big black holes as they appeared to be decorated with color and ornate diamonds. In the Temple I was teaching my students on the properties of herbs and the power of the mind while using astrology and numerology as cosmic tools. I was honored and revered until my fall from grace occurred; I allowed greed, power and corruption to overthrow the purity and integrity of my work. In that lifetime I was buried alive. What is fascinating for me in that scenario is that when it came to choosing a place for our honeymoon, I persuaded my husband to visit Egypt. Once I arrived I had an instant feeling of home. I felt the energy of the place and recognized it. My heart was singing with joy, yes! I was on my honeymoon, but this excitement and feeling of bliss transcended anything I'd ever known before. I never studied history and yet on one particular night of the pub quiz I could answer almost every question relating to ancient Egypt including its many kings and queens. This I now know was vivid recall of past memories. These were stored within my soul library and were reactivated by my trip back to my homeland. The strangest facet of this story is that there was no hypnosis involved, just pure memory activation of a time and place where I once lived.

I was excited and thrilled when I met the renowned psychiatrist Dr. Brian Weiss while attending an "I Can Do It Workshop" in London. Undertaking his lectures was both a revelation and an illumination into the expansiveness of regression therapy. His lifetime of experience proved a direct correlation between past life experiences with present-life fears and phobias that interfere with healthy living. His most significant book *Many Lives, Many Masters* is based on the true story of Catherine, a young 27-year-old patient, who came to him for regression therapy. Dr. Weiss was a conservative professional and was educated to believe that only that which could be scientifically proven was acceptable and real. Through Catherine's revelations he came face to face with the concept of reincarnation. During her many regression states, Catherine recalled detailed past life memories, different places she lived on this earth, both as male and female. *"She recalled vividly the details of each birth, her name, her family, physical appearance, the landscape, and how she was killed through stabbing, by drowning, or illness. And in each lifetime she experiences a myriad of events making progress to fulfill all of the agreements and all of the karmic debts that are owed."* So compelling were her stories that Dr. Weiss began to validate them from the history books. During the course of his treatment with her, Dr. Weiss had an unexpected spiritual awakening that significantly changed his life and the way he viewed death. He went from past life skeptic to past life expert. In Catherine's case her phobias, fears, anxieties and nightmares disappeared after her treatment. This endorses Dr. Weiss's findings and that of other experts that regression therapy frequently leads to cures from physical illness that are carried forward into the present lifetime.

I believe the great physicist Albert Einstein expressed the idea precisely when he said, *"The only thing science is able to prove is that it is unable with certainty to prove anything."*

The research I discovered by psychologist Dr. Helen Wambach was absolutely fascinating. Dr. Wambach was a pioneer amongst others in conducting scientific research into past lives and reincarnation. Wambach had a scientific mind and considered reincarnation and past life memories as sheer fantasy. In the early

1960s she conducted a ten-year study of past life recalls under hypnosis among 1,088 clients. She asked various questions, such as the details of food eaten, clothing worn, time and dates, the answers to which could be verified and aligned with historical, sociological and biological facts. Wambach was able to extract the facts governing the death experience, the reason for birth and the cyclical journey of the soul. Most of her clients reported that their purpose in reincarnation was to learn about love, rather than develop talents or achieve greatness. Others said they had come back to teach humanity humbleness and help develop a higher level of consciousness. Wambach published her findings in books entitled *Reliving Past Lives: The Evidence under Hypnosis* (1978) and *Life Before Life* (1979). It is important to note here that Wambach started out to denounce reincarnation and was a serious skeptic of her time. By the end of her ten-year scientific research she openly admitted that she had become a believer in an afterlife and reincarnation.

The following exercise will activate your memory in believing you were here before.

- Do you have unique gifts that you never trained for and have naturally?
- Have you met a stranger and known instantly – you already know each other?
- Can you speak in a foreign language you feel passionate and excited about?
- Have you been drawn to travel to a particular place – for no particular reason?
- Do you have a yearning to go back to a country because you feel homesick for that place?
- Do you have recurring dreams from which you awake – just as you are about to die?
- Did you fall in love instantly and know he/she is the one?

If you can answer *yes* to some or all of the above, chances are you are delving into some past life memories and this will provide you with a platform to gently explore them.

> *Humankind has not woven the Web of Life; we are but one thread within it. Whatever we do to the web, we do to ourselves. All things are bound together, all things Connect.*
> **Chief Seattle**

NDEs – No one Really Dies – Compelling Evidence that Life Continues

Following my own near-death experience in 1992 (which I discussed earlier), I became obsessed with the phenomenon of near-death experiences or NDEs as they are called in the medical literature. Anyone who has experienced a near-death experience will most certainly believe in the existence of an afterlife. I believe I have already taken part in the journey to the other side. Not only through my NDE but through my meditation practices and out-of-body experiences. Any previous fears I had about death were totally dissolved as I hold a sacred knowing that death is nothing but a graduation from one life to another plane of existence. The vast volume of research undertaken, i.e. medical, scientific, personal experiences and spiritual data, all revealed the same commonalities, for example, floating above their bodies, seeing themselves rising from their beds, watching doctors trying to save their lives, seeing a tunnel, being drawn into a magnificent light, feeling the presence of a holy figure, hearing or seeing a loved one either beckoning them forward or telling them, *"No, it's not your time."* If it was not their time then the person would find themselves being pulled back into the body almost like a thud. This sensation is called catalepsy which means the body has being seized by spirit. (*Smith's Bible Dictionary*)

Reports of near-death experiences are not a new phenomenon.

A great number of them have been recorded over thousands of years. The ancient religious texts such as the Bible, the Koran, and *The Tibetan Book of the Dead* describe experiences of life after death which remarkably resemble modern NDEs. The oldest surviving report on NDE in Western literature comes from the Greek philosopher Plato. He describes an event in his legendary book *Republic*. Plato recounts the story of Er, a soldier who awoke on his funeral pyre and described his journey into the afterlife. This story, however, is not an anecdote for Plato. He integrated at least three key elements of the NDE into his philosophy: (a) the departure of the soul from the cave of shadows to see the light of truth; (b) the flight of the soul to a vision of pure celestial light; (c) its subsequent recollection of the vision of light. The light Er referred to without question is the light most commonly alluded to in today's near-death experience phenomenon. The *Aztec Song of the Dead* is a poetic version of near-death experience recorded by Aztec initiates throughout its ancient civilization. Also, Pope Gregory the Great in the 6th century collected records of near-death experiences as proof of life beyond death. As I mentioned earlier near-death experiences are not a new age phase; NDEs have been recorded and documented for thousands of years, and finally the compelling evidence required in support of the afterlife theory is upon us now.

So what exactly is a near-death experience? Putting it simply, it is a clear and memorable vision that occurs when people are close to death. Researchers now agree that each vision will contain many common elements, such as entering a tunnel, being drawn into a bright light, meeting loved ones in beautiful surroundings, being supported by guides and other angelic beings, being told, *"It's not your time."* Throughout an NDE, hearing and sight become fine-tuned with heightened awareness of everything going on around them. In many cases, it feels as if the vision lasted for hours although the person may have been unconscious only for a brief time. Because of the nature of my work I have met a number of clients who in confidence have told me of their NDE experiences. Interestingly, only one or two had confided in anyone as they feared being ridiculed or disbelieved. One particular client after telling her doctor about her NDE was diagnosed as having a psychiatric illness and ordered to take a vast amount of medication. Needless to say, following a few healing sessions she had no desire to take any form of medication and has since studied in alternative practices. Many books are written about NDEs by doctors and also by survivors themselves. In the following paragraphs I will discuss the findings of several prominent doctors and scientists who at the risk of jeopardizing their own professional reputation added their names to the afterlife phenomenon.

The American mystic Edgar Cayce (1877-1945) otherwise known as the *"Sleeping Prophet"* was able to tap into – what I call – the universal consciousness and awake from these trance states with all the wisdoms and knowledge of technology, science and medicine even though he had no formal training or schooling in any of them. Through NDE visions of the future Cayce foretold the 1929 Stock Market Crash, World Wars I and II, the 1991 Desert Storm War against Iraq and the 9/11 terrorist attacks on America.

In 1975, Dr. Raymond Moody published a book entitled *Life After Life* which describes his study on near-death experiences. Moody recorded and compared the experiences of over 150 patients who died, or almost died, and then recovered. He outlined nine common elements that occur during NDEs which were later supported by Dr. Kenneth Ring.

1. NDEs happen to people of all race, gender, age, education, marital status, social class.
2. Religious orientation is not a factor.
3. People are convinced of the reality of their NDE experience.
4. Drugs do not appear to be a factor.

5. NDEs are not hallucinations.
6. NDEs often involve unparalleled feelings.
7. People lose their fear of death and appreciate life more.
8. People's lives are transformed after having an NDE.
9. People often become psychically gifted after having an NDE experience.

A most remarkable proof of the afterlife came from Dr. Eben Alexander, an American neurosurgeon who suffered a near-fatal case of meningitis that left him in a coma which resulted in an extraordinary NDE. While his body lay in that coma Alexander journeyed beyond this world and encountered an angelic presence who guided him into the deepest realms of heavenly peace and unconditional love. After his miraculous recovery Dr. Alexander (who had been adopted from birth) later discovered that the presence which guided him during his NDE was actually his biological sister, who had died some years earlier. He hadn't known about her until after his recovery. He recognized her in a photograph as the presence that never left him as she guided him while on the other side. Today he is a neurosurgeon who believes that true healing and health can be achieved only when we realize that God and the soul are real, and that death is not the end of physical existence but only a transition. His book entitled *Proof of Heaven: A Neurosurgeon's Journey into the Afterlife* offers the most hardened skeptic compelling proof of an afterlife.

Equally as compelling is *To Heaven and Back: The True Story of a Doctor's Extraordinary Walk with God,* by Dr. Mary Neal. This is another powerful true-life story of what happened as she moved from life to death, to eternal life and back again. Detailing her feelings and surroundings in heaven, her communication with angels and her deep sadness when she realized she could not stay, Dr. Neal shares her captivating experiences of her miraculous survival and the beginning of her spiritual awakening.

Anita Moorjani wrote an inspiring book entitled *Dying to Be*

Me about her near-death experience. Her body was ravaged by malignant tumors and began shutting down. Her vital organs failed and she slipped into a coma and passed over to the other side. Her fascinating journey is vividly recorded, the people she met, and the cause of her cancer; and the choice to return back to the physical plane is intriguing. After returning to her body she made a miraculous recovery with no traces of cancer in her body whatsoever. The experience gave her a whole new perspective on life and how to be that life. Her ultimate and most liberating message, that love is the greatest healer on the planet. Self-worth, self-love and self-acceptance are the key ingredients to a peaceful, happy and healthy life.

Dr. Victor Zammit is a lawyer who presents a most compelling case in support of the afterlife. He is a retired attorney of the Supreme Court of New South Wales and Australia. Due to his psychic and mediumship experiences he began intensive research into the afterlife. His book *A Lawyer Presents the Case for the Afterlife* (1996) provides the most comprehensive scientific evidence for life beyond death. For the extreme skeptic, the evidence given is supported by some of the world's most credible scientists, who without doubt endorse the afterlife phenomenon. Since 2001, Dr. Zammit has offered *"One Million Dollars"* to challenge anyone in the world who can show that the afterlife evidence is not valid. To date the irrefutable objective evidence has failed scientists, physicists and psychologists to provide anything that indicates otherwise. This *"Million Dollar Challenge"* lapses in the year 2025.

Mors Janua Vitae – Death the Gateway to Eternal Life.
Gilbert

Children Experience NDEs – similar to adults

Results from the "Seattle Study" showed that sick children experience NDEs just as much as adults. The report showed that children's near-death experiences were not caused by sedation or drugs but were part of the natural process of dying during their final days. NDEs are indiscriminate and occur across all age groups including young children. Dr. Melvin Morse (1983), an American pediatrician, reviewed many cases of children who had near-death experiences. These experiences had similar features to those of adults, *"feeling peaceful, drawn towards a bright light, floating above the body, communicating with deceased family members, being guided by a presence and being told to go back."* They had vivid recall leaving no room for imagination or fairytale fantasy. What they experienced was similar to that reported by adults, thus leaving no doubt that children do have near-death experiences regardless of religious or cultural backgrounds. In one of Dr. Morse's scientific articles he relates a number of children's NDEs.

One particular story was that of a five-year-old girl whose heart had stopped during surgery. She reported, *"I rose up in the air and saw a man like Jesus because he was nice and he was talking to me. I saw dead people, grandmas and grandpas, and babies waiting to be born. I saw a light like a rainbow which told me who I was and where I should go. Jesus told me it wasn't my time to die."* Another story reported was that of a young six-year-old girl who was critically ill following an episode of meningitis. She reported, *"being out of her body with a sense of being completely free of pain and totally surrounded by love. She reported feeling like a soul neither boy nor girl, neither grown up or child. She felt a sense of peace and completeness. When she looked down, she saw a girl lying in bed."* On reflection she realized she must be that girl, and with that thought she was pushed back into her body. Dr. Morse's research indicates that the vast majority of children who experience cardiac arrest have an NDE. Usually, children who experience NDEs report being given the option of returning to life to be with their family. The reason the child often returns is because it doesn't want to upset or cause sadness to its family.

I dream of a world in which death is no longer feared as being the end of Life, but is seen for what it truly is – The Doorway to Home – and the Entrance to Eternity.

White Feather

Blind People see during NDEs

Dr. Kenneth Ring completed a two-year study into the NDEs of the blind. His findings were published in a book entitled *Mindsight* in which he documented solid evidence of 31 cases where blind people report visually accurate information obtained during an NDE. The best example from his study is that of a 45-year-old woman named Vicki Umipeg. Vicki was born blind. Her optic nerve was completely destroyed at birth because of an excessive amount of oxygen she received while in an incubator. Yet, she was able to see and describe things during her NDE that she never saw before her NDE. Dr. Ring's investigations into the case histories of blind people showed astounding results. Blind people had perfect vision during their near-death experiences, similar to those of sighted persons.

Regardless of their prior attitudes – whether skeptical or deeply religious – and regardless of the many variations in religious beliefs and degrees of skepticism from tolerant disbelief to outspoken atheism – most of these people were convinced that they had been in the presence of some supreme and loving power and had a glimpse of a life yet to come.

Dr. Kenneth Ring

In 2001, Dr. Pim van Lommel, a Dutch cardiologist, conducted a major study into NDEs. He was astounded by the findings his patients exhibited after being pronounced clinically dead. Floating upwards out of their bodies, seeing themselves on the operating table and watching medical teams trying to resuscitate them, being drawn to a tunnel, seeing the most magnificent light, hearing celestial music, feeling of bliss, being in a heavenly place, seeing loved ones and being told, *"It's not your time."* Over 344 patients were involved in Dr. Lommel's study, with most of his patients experiencing some if not all of the above sensations. His work intensified into near-death research, which later became his lifetime vocation. In 2011, *Consciousness Beyond Life: The Science of the Near-Death Experience* was published. Here he provides scientific evidence that the near-death phenomenon is an authentic experience that cannot be attributed to imagination, psychosis, or oxygen deprivation. He further revealed that after such a profound experience, most patients go through a life-changing, often dramatic life evaluation. Further to that, the wisdom gained during the NDE can be life enhancing and have huge positive effects on those who don't have the experience of one. Dr. Lommel shows that consciousness does not always coincide with brain functions, but most significantly that consciousness can be experienced outside of the body. Many of the world's leading experts on the scientific study of death and near-death experiences present compelling evidence from front line medical doctors, care staff and survivors into the ultimate mystery of what happens to human consciousness during the near-death experience. NDEs demonstrate clearly that a consciousness exists beyond the brain and beyond the physical existence. I am humbled to work with dying patients therefore my acceptance of the near-death experience is normal, comforting and enriching. *(The experiences I have witnessed at the bedside of the dying will be discussed in the chapter on deathbed visions.)* I believe a greater understanding of NDEs can not only enhance the way in which we care for the dying but also revolutionize our current world view. I think I will allow Shakespeare to have the last word here.

There are more things in heaven and earth, Horatio, than are dreamt of in your philosophy.
Hamlet 1.5.167-8

What are Out-of-Body Experiences or OBEs?

The phenomenon of out-of-body experience or astral projection is a natural part of the human existence and dates back to ancient times. Professor Susan Blackmore has carried out extensive research in the field of out-of-body experiences and defines the phenomenon as *"an experience in which a person seems to perceive the world from a location outside their physical body."* Different cultures throughout history, Greek, Egyptian, Chinese, and Indian, including the Bible, all contain literature on this phenomenon. They view it as part of life and as natural as breathing. These out-of-body experiences can occur to anybody independent of religion, culture, age, sex, or education. Most out-of-body experiences take place during the night when the body is sleeping, but this can also occur during the day when one blanks out for a few moments. This type of scenario happens to one of my friends all the time. One minute she is communicating with you, and without warning and within seconds she looks completely blank. She is still there in her body, but outside of it. When this happens her soul has decided to check in on someone who she is concerned about, be it a sick child or a family member going through a crisis. As she is a gifted healer, her soul sometimes leaves her body momentarily in order to channel a healing to a client who is in difficulty or in need of healing. This type of OBE is very common and is not harmful to the person experiencing it. I understand that out-of-body or astral projection is a cause for concern with some people as they view it as dabbling and interfering with the unknown. However, it is important to remember that the spirit body is attached to the physical body by a silver cord and remains connected to the body throughout its lifetime until it is broken at the moment of physical death.

(To the trained practitioner, especially Shamans, this cord can be visibly seen.) During a near-death experience (NDE) the spirit body floats above the physical body while remaining connected by the silver cord. However, if it is the divine timing of the soul to leave this earth's plane, the cord disengages from the physical body and death occurs. This is in stark contrast to an out-of-body experience (OBE) whereby the soul can come and go at will. The cord holds the person grounded to earth while the soul takes frequent trips in and out of the body during its lifetime. The cord is a lifeline between the heavens and the earth and is limitless as to how far it can stretch during these out-of-body journeys, with the one major exception being when your time on earth is complete – the silver cord is severed and this is the point of no return.

The Monroe Institute, Virginia, USA is renowned for its experimental and controlled programs on initiating spontaneous out-of-body experiences. Although Robert Monroe passed away in 1995, he left behind a great legacy in the exploration of consciousness beyond the physical body. Thousands of people from all over the world, from all walks of life attend the institute to study many of its programs, in particular out-of-body initiations. The Monroe Institute empowers its participants to awaken to their own true psychic powers and natural gifts. All training is provided in a safe environment, which includes self-induced out-of-body experiments, communicating with loved ones passed and the exploration of past lives. In 1971, Monroe published his first book *Journeys Out of the Body* which to this day remains the bible in out-of-body phenomenon.

Signs of Out-of-Body Experiences

Listed below are a number of signs that may indicate your soul is having an out-of-body experience:

- During sleep you wake up with a feeling of sinking,

floating or suddenly dropping.

- You dream of loved ones and remember having full-blown conversations with them.
- You wake during the night in a state of total paralysis and you can't move.
- You feel a high buzzing vibration particularly around the head area.
- You wake up with the feeling of having been somewhere beautiful and sacred.
- You are prone to daydreaming or staring into space.
- Footsteps or other sounds of a Being's Presence.
- Surge of energy flowing through your body.
- Delightful smell, flowers, perfume, aftershave, aromas.
- You find yourself after falling asleep leaving your physical body.
- You feel at peace after a dream, having met your loved one in spirit.
- You feel a sensation of being pulled back into your body.

It's important for the reader to be aware that most out-of-body experiences occur at night although you may not be consciously aware of it. If you are prone to daydreaming or appear to go blank, this can signify you are having a momentary out-of-body experience. My advice to you is don't panic, trust in the wisdom of your soul as it holds the key to your safety and protection. It will not allow anything to happen to you during these trance states.

Actually, every one of you travels astrally when you go to sleep. Then your Spirit, for the time being, departs from your body, roams into our world and meets souls you love and who have loved you.
Silver Birch

Client's Spontaneous Out-of-Body Experience:
Survival from Abuse

Bobby came to my practice in a last-ditch effort to try and pull his life together before he ended it. Bobby was a managing director of a renowned multinational company. He had worked hard to earn his professional status. As he walked through my door, I could clearly see his energy body was in chaos. It appeared lifeless with little or no energy flowing in, through or around his body. His life force or Chi (Chinese medicine) was blocked. The pain of his past was chiseled and carved onto his face; a lost soul sat before my eyes. His traumatic childhood had finally banged on the door to his heart begging for healing. I had much work to do. It was obvious he was in need of soul retrieval and assistance in the releasing of childhood traumas which were still stored in his body, resulting in toxic overload. While it's important to revisit the past, it's equally important not to re-traumatize the person. Bobby's abuse threw his body and mind into a state of survival. Every day Bobby was reliving his past events and as a consequence was turning on a cascade of stress chemicals, causing an ongoing trauma to his body. By repeatedly recalling his past events, he was unintentionally anchoring his mind and body to the trauma of the past which made it impossible to live in the present. It was important to retrieve Bobby's soul parts and reintegrate the fragments back together. The process began by hearing Bobby's story.

Bobby, at the age of 12, was sent by his parents to boarding college. This was a prestigious college run by religious priests. It was deemed a privilege for anyone who successfully enrolled there. Most students were allocated tasks and his role was to peel vast amounts of potatoes daily for dinner. Peeling potatoes took longer than other duties. Overtime Bobby found himself alone in the kitchen with one particular priest. It didn't take long before an abuse of power was executed. Throughout the session Bobby had vivid recall of specific incidents that happened.

When the abuse was about to begin Bobby's soul would leave his body and not return until after the abuse had ended. He recalled seeing his physical body pushed against a sink – while he was observing the abusive scene from outside his body. This abuse continued for approximately two years until the priest was relocated elsewhere. As a consequence of the abuse, including many flashbacks he suffered with depression most of his life. No matter what medication or what therapist he went to, the depression never left him. His wife who was familiar with my work suggested he come to see me. After all, he had nothing to lose, what was the worst that could happen?

Bobby's Soul Retrieval

Due to Bobby's traumatic past part of his soul fragmented in order to cope with the sexual abuse. I burned sage and created a sacred space while drumming music played in the background. I called forth my spirit guides and those of Bobby's to assist me during this soul retrieval journey. I called forth Bobby's power animal, the Ancestors, the wisdoms of the Ancient Ones to bring healing and restoration to this wounded soul. Taking a few deep breaths my psychic self opened up and I was ready to channel. As his soul was presented before me, I could see a great big chunk of it was missing – instead of a round circle of radiating light, it was damaged and fragmented. After approximately two and a half hours of working on him, it was time to call back the soul parts that Bobby had lost as a young teenager. I always encourage the client to become part of the retrieval process – after all it is their soul retrieval. I invited him to stand tall in a position of power and spiritual mastery and to repeat aloud the following mantra that was appropriate for his healing.

Heavenly Father, Divine Source of all Creation – I, Bobby, Call back my soul parts from all the people, places and situations in my

life in whom I have invested my Spirit. I call back my soul parts from all directions of time – space – and energy. I call back my soul parts from this lifetime – from my abuser who stole my innocence. I call back my soul parts from any other level or plane of existence – consciously or unconsciously known to me. I call my soul parts home to be reunited with my beautiful soul – making me whole – reborn again to new life. I ask this for my highest good, under the law of Grace and the overall enrichment of my soul.
Thank you and it is so. Amen.
Mariel

After the session was complete Bobby said, *"I'm not really sure what happened there but I feel different. I feel the lights have been switched on again. When I came in today all I could see was darkness, now all I see is light."* Shortly after his soul retrieval he reported a decrease and eventual end to his depression. For the first time in his life he felt whole again. He began rebuilding his self-esteem and made healthier life decisions that allowed him to stay present in his body. It took him time to adjust to being fully in his body and learning to love it by adapting new and healthy ways of relating to himself and those around him. Not everyone who comes for soul retrieval has the same instant effect as in the case of Bobby. Some clients are not ready consciously to handle the painful memories associated with the trauma. When this happens I will always respect the uniqueness of where the person is coming from in the knowing that divine timing for the return of the fragmented part must be honored.

Indications of Soul Fragmentation
The following questions are indicators of determining if Soul Loss has occurred:

- Do you suffer from any of the following addictions, i.e. alcohol, sex, drugs, spending or gambling?

- Do you feel detached from your body?
- Do you feel your body does not belong to you?
- Do you find it hard to move forward in life – after your breakup or divorce?
- Do you suffer from anxiety or ongoing depression?
- Do you have suicidal thoughts – thinking the world would be better off without you?
- Do you have a memory loss for certain times in your life?
- Do you suffer from a sleep disorder?
- Do you feel lifeless or dead inside?

If you answered yes to any of the above questions chances are you may be suffering from soul fragmentation. It is important to engage the help of a professional who in a safe environment can retrieve that part or parts of you that withdrew during your traumatic experience.

Throughout my work I have found that various kinds of trauma are responsible for the soul to become fragmented. For example, sex abuse, accidents, loss of loved ones, addictions, surgical procedures, illness, violations and abuse of any kind may leave clients feeling disconnected from their bodies. Soul retrieval is not for everyone; sometimes the client may have a negative attitude towards the process which in turn can block any healing benefits. When I pick up on this type of energy from a client, I encourage them to seek professional help elsewhere to prepare for the soul's return. The soul has a powerful wisdom and supreme intelligence that can find the resources it needs to heal. Always be discerning in whom you entrust yourself to. Make sure the practitioner is registered and upholds ethical standards for best practice procedures. There are many books available on Soul Retrieval, but my favorite is *Shaman, Healer, Sage* by Dr. Alberto Villoldo. My first shamanic training was delivered and received under his mentorship.

The only thing of value in a man is the soul. That is why it is the soul that is given everlasting life, either in the Land of the Sky or in the Underworld. The soul is man's greatest power, it is the soul that makes us human, but how it does so we do not know. Our flesh and blood, our body, is nothing but an envelope about our vital power.

Intinilik, an Utkahikjaling Eskimo

Further Evidence in Support of an Afterlife

I have failed to find that a single person who ridicules the evidence for the Afterlife has given the subject any serious and patient consideration.

Professor William Barrett

Professor Barrett, a Professor of Physics at the Royal College of Science, Dublin, was one of the first to seriously examine the deathbed phenomenon. He became interested in the subject when his wife Florence, an obstetric surgeon, arrived home one evening and told him of a young mother who had died in the hospital that day after giving birth. Just before she died the mother, named Doris, sat up and became very excited about seeing a wonderful place and said that her father had come to take her there. What was equally compelling was the fact that Doris was surprised to see her sister also present with her father. Later it was revealed that the sister had died three weeks earlier, but because Doris was so ill she was not told of her passing. The story was so captivating to Professor Barrett that he undertook a systematic study of deathbed visions. His book *Deathbed Visions* published in 1926 was a summation of his findings, including case studies in which doctors and nurses or relatives present at the bedside of the dying could also see what the dying person saw. Following his findings Barrett said: "*I am personally convinced that the evidence we have published decidedly demonstrates (1) the existence of a spiritual world, (2) survival after death, (3) occasional communication from those who have passed over ... It is, however, hardly possible to convey to others who have not had similar experience an adequate idea of the strength and cumulative force of the evidence that has compelled my belief."* (Society for Psychical Research, June 17th, 1924)

A book entitled *At the Hour of Death* (1977) investigates death and dying with modern research techniques and provides compelling evidence for the survival of consciousness after death. Dr. Osis and Professor Haraldsson carried out extensive research into the mysteries surrounding deathbed visions on a more elaborate scale than Barrett. This was made possible by extensive computer analysis and modern technology which was not available to Barrett. Spanning over a ten-year period they interviewed more than 1,000 doctors and nurses who bore witness to these visions. What these doctors and nurses witnessed could not be explained by psychological, medical, cultural or other form of conditioning. Osis and Haraldsson present compelling evidence that deathbed visions provide the gateway to another existence. Their overall concluding evidence showed that the visions of the dying are not hallucinations brought on by medical interventions in the use of drugs or sedatives, but glimpses through the windows of eternity. As they stated, *"We feel that the total body of information makes possible a fact-based, rational, and therefore realistic belief in life after death."* To date their research provides one of the most authentic and comprehensive works in deathbed phenomenon which will without doubt arouse and stir curiosity within the greatest skeptic.

David Kessler is one of today's most renowned experts on death and dying. He is the coauthor of the best sellers *On Grief and Grieving* and *Life Lessons* with the legendary Dr. Elisabeth Kübler-Ross. His inspiring book entitled *Visions, Trips and Crowded Rooms: Who and What You See Before You Die* is filled with inspirational and intriguing wisdoms around deathbed visions. These reports provide detailed accounts from frontline healthcare workers, medical staff and family members that deathbed visions are extraordinary events witnessed by ordinary people. These fascinating accounts provide a powerful argument that death is not the end and that life continues beyond the veil of death.

The Phenomenon of Deathbed Visions – DBV

I believe no soul is left to wing its viewless flight to Paradise in solitude. I believe the "Gloria in Excelsis" of the shining host of God welcomes the disembodied spirit upon the confines of the new world. I remember hearing once of a little dying child shrinking timidly for the idea of going alone; but just before the end there came a spirit of sublime confidence, a supernatural opening of vision, a recognition of some companionship, and the little one cried out "I am not afraid, they are all here". I believe the chamber of the dying is filled with the holy angels.
Basil Wilberforce

A deathbed vision (DBV) is described as a vision or experience that the individual has before dying. Instances of these unexplained visions have been recorded throughout history and stand as one of the most compelling proofs of life after death. These deathbed visions do not discriminate as they transcend beyond all cultures, age, race, sex and creed. These reported visions may occur at the moment of death or in the days or weeks leading up to death. It is important to note that major commonalities exist between the near-death experience and the end-of-life deathbed vision. The person having a near-death experience is catapulted outside his/her body where he/she meets a loved one or significant other that tells him to *"go back – it's not your time."* This person either by medical intervention or divine dispensation returns to living a normal life again.

In comparison deathbed visions are a determining factor that signals death is close. It's not unusual for the dying person to suddenly gaze upwards with light-filled eyes and exclaim, *"Oh, you have come to take me home."* Usually within a brief time of this happening the person dies. In other words, as mentioned earlier the silver cord is severed from the physical body and the soul is then free to journey onwards; there is no return, life as you know it is ended.

Personal Experiences of Deathbed Visions

When someone passes to my world, you should not think of it as a tragedy for them, but rather as a release from the difficulties experienced. In the world of matter, what for you is a loss – is for us a gain – because it proves once more that death holds no sway over Eternal Life, and that every soul, regardless of its spiritual standing, continues to exist in unbroken sequence.
White Feather

I have witnessed extraordinary phenomenon at the bedside of the dying. I have seen people die with their deceased relatives in the room waiting to take them home. I have seen people fighting with death and terrified of dying when all of a sudden they will open their eyes, gaze into a particular corner of the room, smile and then a sense of peace and calm surrounds them and the fight is no more. One profound feature I have witnessed is the frequent appearance of mothers who appear in deathbed visions. They tend to be the most frequent visitors especially if it's a son or daughter that's about to transition. My mother was no exception to this rule. In the weeks leading up to her passing she would call out to her mother and have little chats. From my experience when the dying person begins calling for their mother it's always an indication that death is very close. Once a concerned neighbor who called to see my mother asked, *"How is your mother doing?"* I simply responded, *"She is waiting in the departure lounge."*

I have seen dying people rise up in bed and call out a name or I've heard words like, *"Ah you've come for me,"* or *"Is that you, Johnny?"* or *"It's so bright, I'm coming soon,"* or *"I'm ready to go now,"* *"Oh the light, the light."* I've also heard the opposite: *"I'm not ready to go yet,"* or *"I don't want to die."* When this happens it usually means they have unfinished business with a family member or someone significant. It often is as simple as waiting for a son/daughter/relative to arrive from another country. Or it may be to make peace with a family member before leaving this world. A lot of healing can happen at the bedside of the dying, and I always encourage families to make their peace with their loved ones and use it as an opportunity to bring closure to the past. This frees the body from any earthly attachments and makes the transitioning phase of the soul easier. From my experience, *love* and *forgiveness* are two of the most precious gifts to offer in the presence of the dying person (this will be discussed later in the book).

Being present at the deathbed of someone you love is a transformational spiritual experience. This is the most significant time as the last moments on earth are treasured. Regardless of the shock and pain of your grief, your primary attention should be focused on the one about to slip into the stillness of death. Oftentimes family members will ask, *"What will I say?"* *"Can he/she hear me?"* *"I haven't spoken to him/her for over forty years,"* *"Can I hold his/her hand?"* etc. My advice is always practical. If you listen reverently with your heart, you will be given the words that are most needed to be heard within the soul of the dying person. Comforting words from a loving voice can provide a temporary shelter before the great silence falls. I have witnessed amazing things around the deathbed experience. I have heard songs sung, prayers shared, stories regaled, forgiveness exchanged, photographs taken, promises made, but the most palpable of all

– remains the strong energy of love that transcends the pain of death. It is an overwhelming blessing to watch a dying person become more beautiful as they approach their final moments. The words spoken between the silent pauses are encapsulated by a newfound freedom and peace. When you gaze upon the dying you can sense they are beginning to belong more fully to the unseen world. It is in these moments that the visions of their departed family members, angels, or holy ones make their presence known. This is a time of incredible beauty where the homecoming for the departing soul is welcomed and handed through the veil into eternal life.

My final hours with Ellie and her Family

I am often called to attend the bedside of the dying. This is a most blessed and humbling request coming from the family of someone who is about to leave this world. Many years ago I was called to the local hospice to attend to one of my clients who was at end of life stage. Prior to her entering the hospice she made her sister promise that in the event of her losing consciousness, I would be called. At this stage Ellie had been in a coma for three days. Back then I was met with a barrage of hostility by the hospice matron. I was questioned, *Who and what was I? What was I going to do to her? Was I going to touch her? Was I going to hurt her?* This ... she said was pure nonsense and totally against the hospice regulations – but they had to respect that I was there at the request of the family. To diffuse her anxiety and calm her down, I kindly invited her to be present while I was performing my work.

Something I had not expected upon entering Ellie's room was to see her entire family surrounding her bed. I had an audience and I sensed they were equally as fretful as the matron. I respectfully explained to the family that I was preparing Ellie's soul for its greatest journey home. After spending some time working on her chakra system (energy points in the body) I felt energy circulating around her heart. To the astonishment of her family Ellie suddenly sat upright and leaned forward. Although I had witnessed many visions, this was one I will cherish forever. Ellie's eyes opened wide as the most inexpressible happiness caressed her face. As she lifted her frail hands upwards into the unknown the most ecstatic and glorious smile enveloped her. This was not simply a smile of unimaginable love, but something far greater beyond it. The veil had lifted between the two worlds and no one present in that room could fail to realize that this was a heavenly sight. Immense peace and serenity filled the room as Ellie lay back on her bed and resumed her comatose state.

I invited her family to approach her one by one and whisper whatever they felt was in their hearts. I assured them that Ellie's sense of hearing was heightened with the understanding that the sound of their voices would be heard by her soul. Within an hour of this happening, I could see Ellie's spirit body rise from her physical body and float upwards. I knew it would not be long before Ellie would take her last breath. This was my time to leave. I hugged each and every one, and made my way out into the eerie corridor. I hadn't gone far when I heard someone shouting, *"Mariel, wait up."* I turned around and there was Ellie's brother with tears pouring down his face wishing to thank me. He said, *"I've never believed in God or anything but something happened in there beyond my understanding that has made me believe there must be something more to life than this and I am grateful these last few hours have proved me wrong."* After a little chat and another big hug I turned and made my way back to the car park. That night Ellie's presence filled my room with light. She looked radiant, healthy and blissful. Just as I called out her name – I awoke, looked at my clock: it read 4:14am. The following morning I received a call from Ellie's sister to say Ellie died at approximately 4:15am last night.

Last Words spoken by Famous People

Mother Teresa, "Jesus, I love you, Jesus, I love you."

Thomas Edison, "It is very beautiful over there."

Nostradamus, "At sunrise, I shall no longer be here."

Sir Walter Raleigh, "I have a long journey to take and must bid the company farewell."

Frederic Chopin, "Now I am at the Source of Blessedness."

J. von Goethe, "More Light."

Michael Landon, "I love you All."

Steve Jobs, "Oh, wow! Oh, wow! Oh! Wow!"

Jack Cash, "He had visions of heaven and Angels."

Florence Nightingale, "Too kind, too kind."

William Wordsworth, "God bless you! Is that you, Dora?"

Daniel Webster, "I still live."

Vincent van Gogh, "Now I want to go home."

Douglas Fairbanks, "I never felt better."

Adam Smith, "I believe we should adjourn this meeting to another place."

Children receive deathbed visions too – similar to adults

Some years ago a young mother came to me for healing. She had lost her 12-year-old daughter three years previously. During the course of her healing I asked her if she believed in an afterlife or something beyond this earth plane. Tears fell down her face as she told me the story of Lucy. At the age of nine, Lucy was diagnosed with leukemia and was very ill. She had a bone marrow transplant that had all the hallmarks of success. After a three-year remission, Lucy's health took a turn for the worst and was given a few weeks to live. A few days before she died, Lucy woke up from a deep sleep and with sheer excitement said to her mother, *"Oh, Mummy – I can't wait to go and play with Peter – he is going to come for me soon and I am to tell you not to be sad for me – cause he's going to take good care of me."* My client had never told Lucy that she had an older brother named Peter who had died two years before she was born. This revelation gave my client some comfort in the knowledge that Lucy's spiritual vision was twofold. Firstly, it brought her son spiritually back to help his little sister make the transition to the other side. Secondly, Peter's appearance to his little sister made it credible for my client to believe in something far greater and profound that exists beyond the veil of death.

Angelic Beings – the Invisible Companions seen around the Deathbed

Angel encounters are widely known and well documented by numerous mystics, artists, poets and visionaries from all walks of life. Ancient texts allow for a greater understanding of who these angelic beings really are and what function they serve towards God and humanity. Some of the most renowned people have endorsed the presence of angels who have inspired their work and guided them throughout life. In *Paradise Lost* (1667) Milton invokes the role of angels in the myth of Adam and Eve. Handel (1685-1759) the great composer said he was influenced by his creator and his angels to compose the *Messiah*. Saint Hildegard of Bingen (1098-1179) a Benedictine Abbess and great mystic wrote numerous texts on angels that were a source of inspiration to future writers. She said, *"Happy angels ... do not part from the love and praise of God."* Sir Isaac Newton, the most famous physicist that ever lived, was a master of gravity and calculus. He used alchemy to understand the physical world and used it to develop his most profound laws, theorems, principles and algorithms. He said, *"These insights were influenced and gifted to him from the angelic realm."* Dante, Goethe, Steiner and Swedenborg all claim to have angel visions that had a profound influence on their work. Finally the famous quote by Michelangelo states, *"I saw an angel in the marble and carved it until I set him free."*

Author Joan Wester Anderson wrote, *"Angels don't submit*

to litmus tests, testify in court, or slide under a microscope for examination." That said, their existence cannot be proved using such measures. You must have a willingness to surrender and open yourself to the possibilities of heavenly beings who over light your every existence since your time of creation. Angels are known as the messengers of God while others believe that they are the thoughts of God. They are with you whether you believe in them or not. Angels are non-denominational and are described in scriptures from all religious backgrounds. The Koran speaks of angels wafting down by the grace of God. The Jewish Kabbalah states that there are 49 million angels. The Bible, Psalm 91, states, *"He shall give his angels charge over thee to keep thee in all thy ways."* Angels are part of Christianity, Judaism, Buddhism, Islam, Hinduism and Taoism. Angels do not belong to any one particular religion and no religion can claim ownership over them. St. Thomas Aquinas states, *"Our Angels were created by God to connect with mankind. While religions were made by mankind to connect with God, angels transcend every religion, every philosophy, and every creed. In fact Angels have no religion as we know it: their existence precedes every religious system that has ever existed on earth."* Religions differ on specifics about angels. Angels are typically depicted in artwork, movies, and stories as humanlike beings with wings, halos, and often glowing in pure golden light. Even Hollywood endorses the concept of angelic beings that walk amongst us. *It's a Wonderful Life* is a (1946) film starring James Stewart as George Bailey who is about to jump from a bridge to end his life. Suddenly his guardian angel Clarence appears and shows him what loss he would be to the town if he ended it all. Growing up I remember being transfixed and glued to the television as *Highway to Heaven* (1984) was aired. Michael Landon played the role of Jonathan Smith, an angel sent from heaven to persuade selfish uncaring people to help one another. In Audrey Hepburn's last film *Always* (1989) she played the role of an angel helping a deceased pilot guide a living pilot to fall in love. The film *Ghost* (1990) was another incredible hit, where the main character Sam Wheat becomes a guardian angel for his wife Molly after he dies tragically. Television and film continue to carry many examples of angelic influences, where miraculous interventions take place under the guidance of these benevolent beings. There is always a moral and central theme to the storyline, i.e. that love is the key and through love all healing is made possible.

However, Hollywood is predominately based on fiction, and I would like to share with you my truths and beliefs about the angelic realms. Angels are divine beings of unconditional love and light. They exist in a much higher vibration than humanity and exist beyond time and space in order to move more freely between the heavens and the earth. The most incredible thing about angels is that they are always ready to step in to guide and support you in a most loving and non-judgmental way. Angels work under divine will, whereas humans operate under free will. Therefore angels cannot intervene in your life unless specifically called upon by you. However, there is one occasion in particular when your angel will step in. If you are in danger of dying and it is not your time to die, your angel will rescue you from sudden death and save you. A wealth of evidence indicates that you are always ministered by angels, especially during times of great sadness around death. Once I was keeping vigil with my friend whose son Jamie was dying from peritonitis. Just before closing his eyes for the last time he said, *"Look, Mummy, there are angels everywhere, all around my bed and one more beautiful than the other."* My friend thinking her son was delirious tried to comfort and rock him. Jamie was insistent, *"See they are right here beside me, I can even touch them."* My friend in the midst of her anguish was struck by Jamie's vision that brought him profound peace and serenity. After Jamie died his vision of angels became a consolation to the entire family. I later confirmed to my friend that I had felt a huge shift in energy in the room as Jamie began to see his angels. While I felt their presence, I also knew they were there to escort Jamie home. Sadly my friend was too overcome with sadness to notice the sheer bliss that Jamie witnessed in those final moments.

From personal experiences it is not uncommon for the dying person to see a loved one, a significant person, angel or a holy person before taking their last breath. Similar stories have come from survivors of near-death experiences that report seeing *"bright beings of light"* or *"angels"* that accompanied them while on the other side. Many people worldwide including doctors, nurses and loved ones report witnessing signs during deathbed visions. They report seeing dying people talking and having full-blown conversations with invisible presences including angels. While some people explain the angel deathbed phenomenon away as hallucinations brought on by medication, I have seen these visions occur when patients are not medicated. According to Johnny Cash's autobiography, his 15-year-old brother Jack suffered a dreadful sawmill accident that left him practically cut in two. On Jack's deathbed, Jack said to his mother that he had visions of heaven and angels, and he wasn't afraid to die. His last words spoken, *"Mother, can you see all the angels around, meet me in heaven."* Moments before Jack died, his family witnessed the whole room light up. Johnny Cash said that Jack never left him and many of his songs were inspired through his connection with his dead brother Jack. Whether you believe in angels or not, throughout time angels have been and continue to be part of the Divine plan. Angels pervade every aspect of life from art, literature, sculpture, paintings, film and now more than ever angels maintain a huge prominence in the music industry. Robbie Williams' career was in decline until he released his most renowned song *Angels*. Abba's *I Have a Dream* contains the powerful chorus: "I believe in angels, something good in everything I see." The Eurythmics sang about an angel playing with "my heart." Kate Bush's album *50 Words for Snow* contains beautiful lyrics in her song *Among Angels*. Paul McCartney said his song *Yesterday* was inspired and gifted to him by angels. How ironic he later called his band Wings. To date no one has invented an angel detector for measuring the presence of angels or spiritual beings. However, enough evidence throughout history endorses and supports the proof of their existence.

> *I am well aware that many will say that no one can possibly speak with spirits and angels so long as he is living in the body, and that many will call it delusion. Some will say that I have spread these ideas around so as to win people's trust, while others will say something different again. But none of this deters me, for I have seen; I have heard; I have felt.*
> **Emanuel Swedenborg, from *Arcana Coelestia* – Heavenly Secrets**

Premonitory Death Vision Experienced by my Oldest Client

> *Death is not extinguishing the light; it is only putting out the lamp because the dawn has come.*
> **Rabindranath Tagore**

Although you may not know or understand the true spiritual meaning of your dreams and premonitions, the fact remains they are more common than you believe. Also they are a source of huge comfort to those about to die and those left behind. Deathbed visions along with a premonition of death are complex experiences and cannot be explained as coming from any one source. I have been around the dying phenomenon for many years now and it is very clear that physical explanations are only part of the experience. They are also life-altering experiences for those who are present to witness them. But for the dying, they appear to lose their fear of death, they are comforted, they are surrounded in peace and die in dignity in the knowing that another journey awaits them. For those who experience an advanced warning or premonition of their death have no fear, but an acceptance that death is not the end as in the case of the two personal stories I will now share.

Barney was one of my oldest clients and was a regular attendee at my night classes and workshops over many years. Barney was 75 years of age and was on a journey of self-discovery. He was raised with very strict religious ideas and for the life of me – I never understood why he kept coming to my classes. He was a very loving man, outspoken and yet had an innate spiritual knowledge that life was far greater than what he was raised to believe. Barney phoned me one day and said, *"Mariel, I'm in a bit of bother, can I come to see you privately?"* Barney had been diagnosed with pancreatic cancer and was given approximately six months to live. Over the coming months my work with Barney was most humbling and insightful. Being a practical man he wanted to get his financial affairs in order, but most of all he wanted to leave this earth without bringing with him the pain and the anguish of his past. Barney came from a rural background in Ireland where the land was almost always left to the oldest son.

We began our journey together towards healing and forgiveness. It was apparent that Barney's resentment and anger lay deeply rooted in the past spanning over a fifty-year period. Barney's story unfolded: he loved the land and he loved to please his father. He worked from dawn to dusk with little or no recognition for his hard work and dedication. Tommy was Barney's oldest brother and showed no interest in the land or its heritage. He already knew he was the successor to the land and didn't have to prove himself. After many years, as Barney put it, *"breaking me backside,"* he decided to leave for England and make a new life for himself beyond the land, beyond Ireland. Barney booked his tickets for the boat and packed a small suitcase to hold his few belongings. On the morning of his departure,

Barney was walking out the gate of his homestead when his father approached him – with begging tears in his eyes pleaded, *"Please don't leave me – what will happen to the land and what will happen to me?"* Barney said, *"Okay, Daddy – sign the farm over to me and I'll stay – Tommy has no interest in it and will run it into the ground."* Barney said, *"Alright, Daddy, I'll stay and don't make me regret it."* Regret he did as his father never kept his word and never signed over the land into Barney's name. After fifteen years he finally left the farm with no inheritance, no money, no pot of gold at the end of the rainbow, nothing but the clothes on his back.

Barney mourned his wasted life, his stupidity at believing his father, and the anger he still held towards his useless brother. We had much work to do as I encouraged Barney to use his energy wisely. Not to use his energy on the past – it was over – but to focus his energy on his own healing and soul purpose. Barney knew his life was slowly ebbing away and wished to make peace with life and everyone and anyone who were part of it – from beginning to end. What turned out to be his final session with me was both exhilarating for Barney and most rewarding for me as his therapist. I was guided by Spirit to take Barney on a journey out of his body into the world of spirit in preparation for his death. This was done in sacred space with my spirit guides in the presence of Barney's guides who were over lighting the entire process. Time appeared endless as a divine energy embraced our space. I felt the presence of Barney's loved ones in attendance. Through them, guidance came through for Barney as to what to do and not to do before his time on earth was complete.

Barney's healing went into a very deep level of his beingness. I knew he was between the two worlds and would return to physical reality when the timing was right for him. After some time Barney opened his radiant eyes and exclaimed, *"Oh Christ, Mariel – I've been in the most beautiful place – I had the best chat ever in my life with me father, he said he was sorry for all the hurt and pain he had caused me. He asked me to forgive him – and asked me to forgive Tommy for his foolishness and make peace with him before I die."* Barney went on to describe the incredible beauty that he saw, fertile land with lakes and mountains like nothing he had ever seen before. He took great delight in telling me he had met his two old sheepdogs Bonnie and Clyde who would also be waiting for him on the other side. He spoke of the most angelic music that his ears had ever heard. Barney said everything was so perfect, so beautiful that he wasn't afraid to die anymore. He said, *"I've seen heaven and I'm going home."* That was the last time I saw Barney. Six weeks later I received a phone call from Barney's wife informing me that Barney had died most peacefully. An emotional reunion took place between the two brothers before Barney died, at last bringing peace and forgiveness to a fifty-year family feud. She said he died with the most serene look glowing across his face. His last words spoken to his family were, *"Godspeed you all till we meet again."*

Now he had departed from this strange world a little ahead of me. That means nothing. People like us, who believe in physics, know that the distinction between past, present and future is only a stubbornly persistent illusion.
Albert Einstein

My youngest brother had a Premonitory Vision of his own death

Joseph was the youngest of seven siblings. He was bright and bubbly with an infectious fun-loving manner. He was highly intuitive and had natural psychic abilities. His passion for saving lives was evident from a very young age. His first ambulance was created from an old car parked up in the back garden. At the age of sixteen he joined the local Red Cross, which became the birthing place for his chosen career in nursing. On obtaining his degree, he followed his heart on a voyage of discovery. He nursed all over the world while gaining many accolades in cutting-edge medical and training disciplines.

Being a free-spirited person it came as no shock to his family when he decided to join the International Red Cross. Much to the heartbreak of my mother he was destined for the Gaza Strip. He told her not to worry, he was taking with him a statue of Our Lady and she would keep him safe. One day while on duty in the Gaza Strip his Red Cross Jeep was caught in a crossfire of shootings. Although his Jeep was riddled with bullets, he and his driver escaped unharmed. Rather than being frightened out of his mind, he said he was fearless and had an immense sense of peace and calm while the bullets ripped in and out through the Jeep. He was convinced and without doubt that on that day they were shielded by a beam of protective light created by Our Lady which insured their safety. Years later, it was the same statue that found its way home to my mother when Joseph died.

Joseph loved life and showed little or no attachment to requiring material things. He had no interest in buying a property or a car, and when questioned he'd say, *"Why do I want a car or a house when I won't live long enough to enjoy them."* My mother loved him very much and truth be known – Joseph was her favorite. After all he was her baby. No matter where he travelled in the world he would always phone home to reassure her he was fine and living it up. Finally, the opportunity of a lifetime came as a post as medical director of Harley Street Clinic in England was offered to him. Without hesitation he seized the moment and relocated to England. It was during this time in England that Joseph became a member of the Spiritualist Church. Through his spiritualist training he learned how to channel his gifts and psychic powers in a more holistic integrative way. He enjoyed the buzz and diversity that England had to offer. At last he felt a sense of belonging and finally had a place to call home.

Joseph made frequent trips back to Ireland. As a family we were no strangers to Irish music. We were raised in a house steeped in music, folklore and dance. Joseph loved coming home and always made a point of gathering the clan together. However, this visit was a little different in that he organized a reunion of cousins that we hadn't met for years. We had a night of fun and laughter with dressing up in costumes of old and laughing till our sides were sore. In one very poignant moment Joseph asked me to sing *Amazing Grace*; this was his favorite song. Joseph sat on the floor beside me as I reluctantly cleared my throat of many cobwebs. I was rusty as I hadn't sung in years. Afterwards, as Joseph and I made our way down the hallway, he suddenly stopped, placed his hands on my shoulders and said, *"Something is going to happen before this summer is out and it's going to change the whole dynamics of our family."* With that I said, *"Joseph, how many gins did you have?"* He smiled and said, *"Mariel, I'm so sad – yet I'm so happy – I'm not sure what it is but I will know more when it comes nearer the time."* I'll never forget how beautiful his eyes looked as he grabbed my arm, swung me around the hallway and said, *"I love you."*

The following morning Joseph kissed everyone goodbye and left for the airport. Little did I realize then that was going to be the last time I would ever see him alive. Two weeks later, Joseph died of an aortic aneurysm, no warning, just gone within the blink of an eye. He was 36 years old. His funeral brought friends from all over the world who wished to pay their respects to a loyal friend and professional colleague. This brought great comfort to my mother and to us as a family. The Red Cross flag was draped across Joseph's coffin and was presented to my mother at his graveside. Joseph had a premonition of his death, but the details of its timing were clouded. However, on this occasion there was a grace in not knowing the eternal outcome. Whenever I hear *Amazing Grace* I know Joseph is near sending his love and guiding me on my spirit path.

Amongst my brother's belongings my sister found this poem in his bedside locker. He was very poetic and most creative. I believe the words written foretell his imminent death.

My Brother Joseph's Poem

When winter mist hangs still and frost invites a chill. When days are short and dark and trees stand grey and stark. When life's depressed and dull, and spirits seem to lull – this time – this time of waiting time between despair and hope – this in-between time of expectation. Time of learning to cope, waiting for mist to rise from troubled hearts. Frost to clear from numbed hearts and minds. This precious time before the Savior comes. Then suddenly but gently like sunlight peering through the greyness of our life – You are there, You, your beauty and the beauty of God within.
Joseph J. Forde

After Death Communication – ADC

Death is a stripping away of all that is not you. The secret of life is to "die before you die" and find that there is no death.
Eckhart Tolle

After death communication is an ancient and recurring theme that is well documented in the folklore and literature of every culture worldwide including religious texts such as the Bible. The first scientific studies were published in 1894 by the Society for Psychical Proceedings, England. Altogether there were 32,000 cases of after death communications recorded. Further studies were carried out by researcher Camille Flammarion who compiled thousands of cases in his books *The Unknown* (1900) and *Death and Its Mystery* (1925). The researchers found that many people in every country irrespective of age, gender, religion or economic background experienced after death communications. Their findings present persuasive evidence that ADCs are authentic contacts from deceased loved ones.

After death communication occurs when a deceased loved one makes direct contact with a living person. This can happen through dreams, meditative states or out-of-body experiences. Many famous people, including President Abraham Lincoln, Charles Dickens, Sir Arthur Conan Doyle, Winston Churchill, Paul McCartney and Robbie Williams, all claim they received visits from their departed loved ones. The eminent psychiatrist Carl Jung related a personal after death dream he had: *"Six weeks after his death my father appeared to me in a dream ... It was an unforgettable experience, and it forced me for the first time to think about life after death."* Jung was a Swiss psychiatrist with a theoretic mind; making the above statement would have left him exposed to ridicule. However, his experience was so profound he felt compelled to share it.

Swedenborg Case – Swedenborg Contacts Countess's dead husband over Receipt

Emanuel Swedenborg was known as the greatest scientist of all times. He was a genius and great mystic who explored the mystery of the afterlife. At the age of 55 years he had a series of clairvoyant visions, which he said, *"gave [him] the ability to experience the spiritual dimensions."* He claimed to have conversed with biblical prophets, apostles, Aristotle, Socrates and Caesar, including many of his friends who maintained continuous contact after their deaths. In 1761, the Countess de Marteville went to Swedenborg in the hope that he could help her find a lost receipt. The Countess was given a very valuable silver necklace by her husband before he died. The silversmith was demanding an exorbitant payment from the Countess for the necklace, saying her husband had not paid for the valuable piece. The Countess could not find the receipt and asked Swedenborg to contact her dead husband and ask him about it. Three days later Swedenborg told the Countess he had made contact with her husband in the spirit world. Her deceased husband informed Swedenborg that the receipt was in a writing bureau upstairs. The Countess said she had already searched the bureau and there was no receipt to be found. Swedenborg, following her dead husband's advice, told the Countess to remove a certain drawer and pull off a false section from the back. The Countess did as requested and there in a secret compartment was the receipt for the necklace. This compartment was only known by the dead count. This story was validated by 11 different sources and endorsed by Swedenborg himself when he was later questioned about it. There are many gifted spirit mediums that can make contact and converse with crossed-over souls.

May I offer a word of caution here: always use discernment in choosing a medium or psychic person for the purpose of afterlife contact with a loved one. Research their authenticity and make sure they come well recommended by others who have tried and tested their credibility and genuineness.

Dr. Elisabeth Kübler-Ross encounters patient who died ten months earlier

There are varied ways in which a deceased loved one can make contact with a living person. Sometimes, a silhouette or outline of the deceased person can be seen by the individual. Oftentimes, their appearance is to bring an important message to a person in times of great challenge or in great distress, or to save them from harm. One such case was that of Elisabeth Kübler-Ross, the gifted psychiatrist who pioneered the study of death and dying. Dr. Kübler-Ross claimed that a former patient of hers appeared to her when she was thinking of giving up her investigative work into the death and dying phenomenon. Dr. Kübler-Ross had been feeling discouraged about her research with the dying because of the opposition and hostility she encountered from her colleagues. It was very late in the evening as Dr. Kübler-Ross left the lecture hall and made her way to the elevator. The woman, Mrs. Schwartz, got into the lift and accompanied her all the way along the corridor into her office. Dr. Kübler-Ross said it was the turning point in her work as a medical doctor when the deceased patient materialized before her like a translucent figure. Mrs. Schwartz told Dr. Kübler-Ross not to give up her work as her mission and purpose had just begun. Dr. Kübler-Ross thought she must be hallucinating because the woman she recognized as Mrs. Schwartz had died ten months earlier. Then Dr. Kübler-Ross asked her to write her name and the date down on a piece of paper and sign it. Before doing so, Mrs. Schwartz asked Dr. Kübler-Ross, *"to promise her that she would not abandon her work because life after death was a reality and the world needed to know it."* Eventually when Dr. Kübler-Ross said, *"I promise,"* Mrs. Schwartz disappeared. It was later established that the handwriting was the authentic hand of Mrs. Schwartz, who had also written the current date on the paper – ten months after her death.

Death is simply a shedding of the physical body, like the butterfly coming out of a cocoon.
Elisabeth Kübler-Ross

Dead husband saves his young wife

In some cases deceased loved ones can appear with the express purpose of saving loved ones from danger. This happened to Elaine Worrell who lived with her husband on the top floor of an apartment building in Iowa. One day Elaine saw a young man in her hallway who beckoned her to follow him downstairs into the apartment of a young widow. The young woman was unconscious on the bed after having slashed her wrists. When the young widow recovered, she showed Elaine a photograph of her late husband. Elaine recognized it immediately as the young man who had led her downstairs into his wife's apartment. His appearance to Elaine prevented his wife's imminent suicide. (Holzer 1963: 138-141)

My father saved me from ending my Life: Personal After Death Communication

I have always believed in the concept that *"seeing is believing."* Having said that, I know the Divine has placed many visions before me in order to satisfy my curiosity around my psychic gifts and beliefs in the afterlife. My doubting Thomas syndrome has served me well. I no longer need to put my hands in the wounds of the crucified Christ to believe in the visions and messages I receive from loved ones deceased. I have seen and I believe. It's a privilege and a most sacred experience to be a witness to such immortality. These visions have expanded my understanding of life, death and life after death. While I have experienced many after death communications from deceased loved ones – there are many I could share but for now the most life-altering one was that with my own deceased father.

As previously mentioned, I survived cervical cancer, but what I could not survive was the brokenness of my marriage. I had no love, no purpose, no meaning, no dreams to fulfill, nowhere to escape the pain and sadness that imprisoned my troubled soul. My despair and anguish turned to hopelessness as I fell deeper into the abyss of darkness. The darkest night of my soul was placed before me as I decided to end it all. I remember the coldness of that January night and my final surrender that would bring me the peace I so yearned for. I had endured numerous traumatic events that would now act as a catalyst for that one fatal moment to end my life. It was after 2am, when in a state of revengeful madness I found the keys to my husband's new car. In brokenness I wandered towards my front door. I had a plan. I was going to drive myself and his new car into the docklands. Many suicides had taken place at that spot due to the fact that there were no protective barriers in place at that time. It felt so simple and easy ... all I had to do was close my eyes ... drive real fast ... put my foot on the accelerator and it would all be over. However, the Divine had other plans for me. Just as I tried to open my front door my father's face appeared on the panel. His hand went up in front of me signaling me to *"STOP,"* and with a smile on his gentle face said, *"Maulie a cudeen, keep your powder dry."* (This was my father's pet name for me.) The most brilliant golden light particles radiated and swirled all around his head. I stood there totally transfixed. I could hear and feel the most beautiful sound of heavenly music. My heart swelled in this love as a wave of serenity engulfed my soul. Just as I reached out to touch him – he disappeared.

But I will never forget the overwhelming sense of peace and love that caressed and soothed my soul that night. Was I crazy, had I totally lost my mind or did my father in spirit come back to save me? The answer is yes, he did. My leaving would have been premature and my mission on earth incomplete. My challenge was to overcome the memory of a suicide from a previous lifetime where I ignored and denied my natural gifts and psychic abilities. Being saved in this lifetime afforded me the opportunity to redress my past life memory and create a more holistic and integrative one in my present lifetime. I was given a second chance to share my gifts with the world without fear or condemnation. After the dissolution of my marriage, it took many years of intense healing to finally retrieve my soul and gain freedom from the wounds of my past. I now know I was saved in order to honor my psychic gifts and use them for the overall well-being of others.

From what I now know and understand from the Spirit world suicide is never planned prior to birth as a certainty. But it is often planned as a possibility similar to my situation. Every suicide preventable by divine intervention is prevented. For example, the amount of times I've heard the suicidal person say, I was just about to pull the trigger when a bird flew past my head and distracted me, or I was just about to jump when someone called out my name, or I had the tablets in my hand when the phone just rang and startled me. All the above are what I call interventions

– where something or someone will step in at the exact moment to prevent the suicide from happening. If you have lost a loved one to suicide, please know there was nothing you could have done to save them. It was their time to exit, heartbreaking and all as it is for those left behind. (Suicide will be discussed in detail in a later chapter.)

The owl whose night-bound eyes are blind unto the day, cannot unveil the mystery of light. If you would indeed behold the spirit of death, open your heart wide unto the body of life. For life and death are one even as the river and the sea are one. Trust in your dreams for within them is hidden the Gate to Eternity.
The Prophet Kahlil Gibran

Pay Attention to your Dreams: They are Sacred Love Messages

I believe that dreams are one of the most mysterious and fascinating parts of the human experience. Psychologists such as Carl Jung and Sigmund Freud tried to interpret dreams and the subconscious mind. Their research yielded many theories including vast amounts of data in relation to dream interpretation. They were by no means the first to undertake this elusive topic. Dream interpretation has directly influenced Native American culture and spiritual beliefs for centuries. They believe their dreams influence the conscious soul of the dreamer to usher in positive change and transformation. The Native Americans honor the wisdom of their dreams. They hold them very close in their hearts. They have never forgotten how the Great White Spirit moves and communicates to them during sleep states. Dreams enable them to have complete objectivity in finding their way in life, not only in the inner world but also in their outer world of nature. Their dreams can foretell the weather and provide invaluable guidance in their hunting, upon which their livelihood is dependent. The dreamcatcher is rooted deeply in symbolism and has many spiritual connotations. They believe that the night air is filled with dreams both good and bad. The dreamcatcher collects the bad dreams while the good dreams gently fall upon the mind of the sleeping person. The circular shape represents the circle of life, with no beginning and no end. This is significant to many Native Americans because they believe that death is part of life and that the spirit lives on beyond death.

Everyone dreams whether they are aware of it or not. Dreams usually happen when the mind is in an egoless state where the rational mind rests during sleep. When you sleep you allow your loved one to enter your world of dreams. This is the meeting place between the two worlds. Your dreams are the catalyst for messages to come through from your loved one in spirit. Meeting your loved one in your dreams provides a temporary sanctuary for healing your grief. It offers proof that even after death your loved one lives on and wishes to communicate with you. Regular dreams can be fragmented and are easily forgotten. You awake in the morning confused about the details and you can't remember if it was real or just a dream. By contrast a visitation dream is real, it is an unforgettable experience. You feel your loved one's presence and have vivid recall of the entire conversation that took place. A dream visitation is so significant that you will probably remember it for the rest of your life. Visitation dreams are more common than people realize but sadly they are often dismissed or not talked about out of fear of having their sanity or credibility questioned.

Personal experience of Dream Visitation: My Father to the Rescue

After the breakup of my marriage I found it hard to find peaceful sleep. My sense of fear and danger was ultra-vigilant. One particular night I woke with the onset of a major panic attack. It was so overwhelming that I could not breathe. I was gasping for breath and was so traumatized that I could not lift myself up. I lay paralyzed as I struggled to catch a breath. The tears poured down my face as I felt I was going to die. Then miraculously my father appeared and sat at the end of my bed. A halo of light surrounded his head. He wore a white shirt with a baby blue cardigan over it. He said, *"You're all right now, Maulie, and I'm here to mind you."* After some time my breathing returned to normal and I sat up in bed. I said, *"Daddy, you need a haircut."* Just as I leaned over to switch on the bedside light he was gone. I knew my father's visit was no figment of my imagination. It was real; it was a face-to-face visit with my deceased father. Once again he came to save me in my hour of great turmoil. I remember every detail of it, from the colors around him to the feeling of pure unconditional love. This energy of love filled every fiber of my being. I felt a peace and serenity that comforted me with the ultimate knowing that my father in spirit continues to protect and watch over me.

Some of my clients have reported their deceased loved ones appearing to them in dreams and providing them with valuable information regarding wills, selling of property, finding valuable items, approval of new relationships, financial and legal guidance. Dream messages are usually straight to the point with a very clear message on where to find the missing items. One lady recounted the story of her deceased husband coming to her in a dream and telling her where to find the title deeds of the farm. Without these deeds she was destined to lose her home and her farm which was handed down through three generations. Honor your dreams and learn to interpret the hidden meanings they contain, because when you least expect it your dreams may hold the key to your infinite possibilities.

Gentle Exercise: Know that your Loved One can hear and communicate with you. All you need do is, say their name out loud, sense and feel the connection of love, know whatever you wish to say from your heart, your Loved One receives it through their spirit heart.

Heavenly Signs: your Loved One is trying to Contact You

It is well documented that many people from all over the world and all walks of life believe they have been contacted by their deceased loved one in spirit. Know that your loved one will try to communicate with you through messages, signs and other subtle signals. One of the most modern inspirational books on after death communication is *Hello from Heaven* by Bill and Judy Guggenheim. Their groundbreaking research of ADCs confirms that love is eternal and communication does not end with physical death. Their research documents many such experiences stating that after death contact is a normal and acceptable part of the grieving and healing process.

It is not unusual for a friend to say, *"Call me when you get there,"* or *"I'll call you when I get home."* This is a normal exchange of words by anyone leaving home and taking a journey by car, plane, train or bus. It is only natural when you get to your final destination that you make that call as promised to say, *"I've arrived okay."* Now your loved one has arrived on the other side and asks you to be aware of the many signs that will be placed before you as reminders that your loved one is watching over you. These signs will come in a variety of ways and the key is to keep an open mind to the synchronicities that are placed before you. Have you at any point wondered if your loved one is trying to make contact with you?

The following are the most common signs that your loved one is drawing close to you.

Sensing their Presence

Many people report sensing the presence of their loved one after their passing in a very positive and reassuring way. You may notice a change or shift in energy or the temperature suddenly going from warm to cold or vice versa. You may feel like someone is sitting next to you while you watch TV or work on your laptop. You feel their love, their presence watching over you although you cannot see them physically.

Feeling their Touch

Oftentimes during tremendous grief your loved one will endeavor to make their presence felt. Feeling your loved one's touch is most common in the days following their passing.

You may feel your loved one gently touch your hair, hold your hand, pat you on the shoulder, or you may even feel an affectionate embrace. If this happens do not discount the feelings as they are true signs that your loved one is letting you know they are okay and want you to be too.

Smelling their Fragrance

You can often tell when your loved one is checking in on you by the various smells associated with them. For example, my father smoked a pipe and for months after his passing and with no logical explanation I could smell his pipe in certain parts of my home. Even now, many years later I know he's visiting because the smell of his pipe runs through the house. These visits happen always on the occasions that were most significant to him like Father's Day and Christmas Eve. For no reason if you smell the fragrance of your loved one's perfume, aftershave lotion, flowers or favorite food trust it's a sign that your loved one is nearby or present.

Hearing their Voice

Your loved one communicates to you through your thoughts. Because your loved one no longer has a physical body, it is more likely that your loved one will speak to you telepathically. In other words, they will be sending their thoughts to you. These thoughts will just pop into your head for no reason, maybe a picture of your loved one, an event, a special date or time of day will come into your consciousness unexpectedly. The more you become aware that your loved one is speaking to you telepathically, the more they will continue to reveal themselves to you through this telepathic channel. Always remember your loved one is just a thought away.

Unexpected Electrical Activity

Most of the time when the electricity goes mysteriously askew in your home, it is often your loved one attempting to gain your attention and let you know they are present. Everything is made up of energy and it's easy for energy to be manipulated through electrical appliances. There are a number of ways they can do this, like lights flickering on and off, turning the television volume up or down, alarm clocks going off, bulbs blowing, phone ringing from an unknown number and when you answer it – there is only static on the line, no one on the other end. It is also common for the doorbell to ring; you go to answer it to find no one there. When these types of things occur out of the blue with seemingly no explanation, this means a loved one is attempting to gain your attention and let you know they are present.

Dreams and Visitations

Dreams are one of the most common ways in which your loved one in spirit can communicate to you. As I mentioned earlier dreams are the meeting place between the two worlds. When your loved one appears in your dreams there can be a number of significant reasons for this encounter. They may have an important message that they wish to impart to you. They may have answers to questions you've been searching for. They may want to comfort you in your grief. They also visit to acknowledge significant events such as births, weddings and anniversaries. Sometimes they appear in your dreams before the passing of a significant other to let you know they will be there to take them into the light. Or they may just wish to check in with you from time to time to see how you are doing.

Symbols, Signs, Coins: Communication from your Loved One

If you find different things showing up out of blue, you may like to do some research on *"Apports"* (gifts from spirit) where objects appear before you from nowhere. Symbols like feathers, pennies, stones, and small objects that have significance to either you or your loved one will turn up when you least expect it. Other signs can appear in the form of repeating numbers. You may see the same numbers flashing on your alarm clock, or the same numbers on a number plate of a car, or the same numbers appearing on your phone. You may relate a number sequence to a particular time or date when your loved one passed. You will see the same number over and over again until you get the meaning of their message. Your loved one can also use music or songs to trigger memories or events for you. Sometimes you may wake up with a song or tune playing over and over in your head and you have no idea why you are thinking of it. Or perhaps you turn on the radio and the same song is playing over the airways. My advice is to pay close attention to the lyrics, there could be a valuable message in it for you from your loved one. These synchronicities are signs of confirmation that your loved one is only a thought away.

Rainbows are Heaven's Calling Card

Rainbows are used symbolically in mythology, folklore, religion and the arts. The mystical rainbow is considered to create a pathway between heaven and earth, bringing peace and tranquility to the observer. When you see a double rainbow it symbolizes transformation and new beginnings. According to Chinese mythology a single rainbow signifies a new soul descending from heaven to earth while in contrast a double rainbow represents the movement from earth to heaven – a sign that your loved one has made it to its heavenly home. So when you see a majestic rainbow know that your loved one is thinking of you and reminding you that this rainbow is your bridge of hope and a promise of something greater to come. Your loved one will always find ways for you to feel their presence and sense their eternal love.

Orbs of Loved Ones appearing in Digital Photographs

Spirit orbs can now be captured in digital photographs. They appear as balls of brilliant colored spheres of light. A growing number of people are now experiencing the orb phenomena as a spiritual and sacred connection after the death of a loved one. Orbs have been reported during OBEs and NDEs with the most publicized being the brilliant orb of light in *Proof of Heaven: A Neurosurgeon's Journey into the Afterlife*, by Dr. Eben Alexander. He states that a young woman accompanied him during his near-death experience. She appeared not only in human form, but in the form of a brilliant orb of light. She was later identified through a family photograph as his sister who had died ten years before Alexander was born. The spiritual magic contained within orbs is pure consciousness. Orbs are the most readily available proof of the existence of life beyond the veil of death. Thanks to digital technology, you now have a visual experience that possibly validates for the first time what mystics and sages have expressed for millennia – that life is eternal, that you are an eternal being.

Reasons why your Loved One cannot get through to you

Your loved one in spirit will try endlessly to let you know that they are happy and reside in another plane of existence. Even as they attempt to communicate with you, there are a number of reasons that may block their messages getting through to you.

- If you feel that your grief is unbearable – know that your sadness creates a wall of depression around your heart which makes it impossible even for the strongest of spirits to penetrate. When your grief begins to subside and your heart opens – only then can your loved one get through to you – pay attention to the signs.
- If you experienced a meaningful dream or received a symbol, but instead of holding it as a sign from your loved one – you passed if off as a coincidence or completely ignored the message it conveyed.
- If you have unresolved resentment, guilt, or anger towards your loved one that will automatically shut down any chance of your loved one penetrating through the field of negativity where your anger resides. Once you are in a space of love and forgiveness, and with patience, you will get the messages you were intended to receive.
- If you place demands or expect too much from your loved one that too will block communication. For example, *"If you are here, turn the lights on and off,"* or *"Switch the channels on the TV,"* or *"Make the telephone ring."* Your loved one can do many things, but they don't suddenly gain superpowers when they die. Allow your loved one to choose the communication that is best suited to you and have faith that the messages will come at the right time in a meaningful way.
- If you are too traumatized by your grief your loved one may decide to first communicate with a relative or close friend instead of you. Your first reaction is, *"Why didn't he/she contact me first?"* The answer quite simply is – your loved one in spirit definitely wishes you to know that he/she is okay and chooses to appear to the person who is most receptive to get the message to you at that time.

Why should I be out of mind because I am out of sight? I am but waiting for you, for an interval somewhere very near, just around the corner.

Henry Scott Holland

Beautiful Exercise: Creating a Sacred Heartlink to connect with your Loved One

Your loved one knows you wish to communicate with them and asks you to be patient with the process. Right now your grief is so painful that it is difficult to reach you through the ocean of tears. Your loved one sends you messages of love and hope, and reassures you that death is only a transition, a moving from one place to another, almost like moving house.

To begin with, if it feels right for you – light a candle in honor of your loved one.

Play some gentle music in the background, as the vibration of the music will lift your heart energy away from grief into the energy of love.

Open your heart and bring the image of your loved one to mind. Recall a special memory where your loved one was happy, healthy and full of laughter. As you activate these memories you are making it easier to attract your loved one's energies into your consciousness.

Allow a feeling of peace and calm to enfold your body. If you wish you may be drawn to sit quietly in your loved one's favorite chair or couch. Maybe you are guided to wrap a jumper or cardigan belonging to your loved one around you. Close your eyes and in your own time ask your loved one to draw close to you. When the image of your loved one comes before you, visualize a beautiful golden stream of light flowing gently from your heart to the heart area of your loved one.

Now concentrate on your breathing; as you breathe out send your love along the beam of golden light from your heart to the heart of your loved one. As you breathe in your loved one will be sending their love along the golden beam of light from their heart to your heart.

As you focus on your breathing and with each in- and out-breath your heart-to-heart connection intensifies. Your loved one in spirit will feel the love you are sending instantly, and will immediately return unconditional love back to you.

In this sacred space you can ask your loved one any question or worries that may be on your mind since they passed. Listen to the inner promptings that come to your mind. Allow in whatever messages you hear or whatever images that may be placed before you. Feel the loving energy of your loved one as it guides and comforts you in tenderness.

Rest awhile in the essence and energy of pure love. Feel the heartlink between the shores of your souls become one. Feel the infusion of divine love, blessings and healing light as it flows all around you engulfing you in peace and serenity. Allow time to bathe in this sacred healing love.

When you feel it's time to disconnect the energetic heartlink between you and your loved one, take comfort in the knowing that you can reactivate this sacred connection anytime you choose. Through the stillness of your heart a two-way communication can exist between the heavens and the earth. Say thank you for the experience and bless the connection that occurred, until you reactivate the heartlink again.

Loving Message from your Loved One:
I will always remain connected to you and to those I love beyond the veil of death. Love transcends beyond all boundaries, all time, all space and energy. Love is the language my soul sends to you now from my heavenly home.
Mariel

A Powerful Parable of Life after Delivery: Death/ Rebirth/Existence

Before I conclude this section of the book there is a powerful thought-provoking conversation that takes place between twin boys in their mother's womb before birth. According to the late Wayne Dyer, the original story was told by Henri JM Nouwen. However, it appears the parable originated earlier in the writings of Pablo Molinero. Just for a moment imagine that the twins possess two very different viewpoints of their world. One accepts the existence of a life beyond the walls of the womb. The other believes that nothing exists beyond life within the womb. This scenario can be compared to the existence or nonexistence of life beyond death. *"Is there life beyond the womb?"* can be equated to posing the question, *"Is there life after death?"* This parable forms the blueprint for questions and answers that are held in the hearts of those seeking validation of an afterlife. I believe this parable gives birth to the seed of eternity within the womb to the advancing immortality of the soul in an afterlife.

Conversation in the Womb: A Parable of Life after Delivery

Once upon a time, a set of twins were conceived in their mother's womb, weeks passed, and the twins developed. As their awareness grew they laughed for joy, "Isn't it great that we were conceived? Isn't it great to be alive?" Together the twins explored their world. When they found their mother's cord that gave them life they sang for joy, "How great is our mother's love that she shares her own life with us." As the weeks stretched into months the twins noticed how much each was changing.

"What does this mean?" asked the first. "It means that our stay in this world is drawing to an end," said the second. "But I don't want to go," said the first. "I want to stay here always." "We have no choice," said the second, "but maybe there is life after birth!"

"But how can it be?" responded the first. "We will shed our life cord, and how is life possible without it? Besides, we have seen evidence that others were here before us and none of them have returned to tell us that there is life after birth."

And so the first fell into deep despair saying, "If conception ends with birth, what is the purpose of life in the womb? It is meaningless! Maybe there is no mother at all." "But there has to be," protested the second. "How else did we get here? How do we remain alive?" "Have you even seen our mother?" said the first. "Maybe she lives in our minds. Maybe we made her up because the idea made us feel good." The first continued, "You actually believe in Mother? That's laughable. If Mother exists then where is she now?" The second replied, "She is all around us. We are surrounded by her. We are of her. It is in Her that we live. Without her this world would not and could not exist."

Thus, while the first raved and despaired, the second resigned himself to birth. He placed his hand in the trust of the mother. "How can there be life after birth?" cried the first. "Do we not shed our life cord and also the blood tissue when we are born? Have you ever talked with someone who was born? Has anyone ever reentered the womb after birth to describe what birth is like? NO!" As he spoke, he fell into despair, and in his despair he moaned, "If the purpose of conception and our growth inside the womb is to end in birth, then truly our life is senseless." He clutched his precious life cord to his breast and said, "And if this is so, and life is absurd, then there really can be no Mother."

"But there is Mother," protested the second. "Who else gave us nourishment? Who else created this world for us?" "We get our nourishment from this cord — and the world has always been here!" said the first.

"And if there is Mother, where is she? Have you ever seen her? Does she ever talk to you? NO! We invented the idea of the mother because it satisfied a need in us. It made us feel secure and happy."

The second replied, "Sometimes, when you're in silence and you *focus and you really listen, you can perceive her presence, and you can hear her loving voice, calling down from above."*

And so the last days in the mother's womb were filled with thousands of questions and a great fear. They both knew their birth was at hand, and they both feared what they did not know. Suddenly the womb burst open and the first is born, the second moments later. They cried as they were born into the light. They coughed out fluid and gasped the dry air. And when they were sure they had been born they opened their eyes – seeing life after birth for the very first time. They say what they yet did not understand as they found themselves cradled lovingly in their mother's arms. They lay awestruck before the beauty and truth that they a few minutes before could only dream to know.

Pablo Molinero

In summary of Part 1 of this book, it is my greatest wish that the reader will take refuge in the knowledge presented to validate the existence of an afterlife. It has taken me years to come out of the shadows and into the light of my soul to share my experiences and unwavering belief in a life beyond this earth's plane. I have witnessed unbelievable phenomena that are beyond the reality of this physical world. What I have seen is undeniably profound, but incredibly real. I can honestly say that I have crossed the threshold of skepticism into the world of immortality where the soul is eternal and survives beyond physical death.

Part 2: Navigating the Uncharted Waters of Grief

Every soul is immortal for whatever is in perpetual motion is immortal. Every man's soul has by the law of his birth been a spectator of eternal truth, or it would never have passed into this our mortal frame, yet still it is no easy matter for all to be reminded of their past by their present existence.
Plato

Part 2 of this book offers you a spiritual connection to your loved one in spirit by providing the reader with techniques to use as coping skills. Included are channeled affirmations for the reader to use as empowerment tools enabling a two-way communication between you and your loved one. Also included is a valuable guide on how to help children navigate through the grieving process. Children do not have the resources or experiences to verbalize how they are feeling or what is on their minds. These techniques provide a platform for children to express their grief in a healthy and creative way.

The primary stages of grief will be identified using them as a framework in your grieving process. Bear in mind your grief is personal and individual to you. There is no right or wrong way to grieve. Grieving is a process, it takes time; it cannot be rushed, forced or hurried. There is no timetable or exact date for your grieving to stop. Be patient with yourself and allow the process to naturally unfold.

Also included are a series of exercises – that enables the

reader to identify where they are presently at in the grieving/ healing process.

Throughout this part of the book you will embrace a knowing that death is a transition, a mere shedding of the physical body with the understanding that the soul is immortal and that part of you that never dies. Within the process of birth or death, the soul has its own unique timing. Whether entering life at birth with the in-breath, or exiting life in death with the out-breath, the soul chooses its timing, a time to be born and a time to die.

Death is the greatest fear that exists within the universe. It is the ultimate vulnerability that brings mankind to its knees. Death brings finality to the world. It unravels a unique tapestry of love, feelings, emotions, sadness and fears. Then it all falls apart like a piece of a knitted garment unraveling stitch by stitch during the process of dying. How you deal with grief and loss will depend on many factors, including your coping style, your personality type, your life experiences, your belief system and how significant the loss is to you.

> *The most beautiful thing we can experience is the Mysterious. It is the source of all true art and all science. He to whom this emotion is a stranger who can no longer pause to wonder and stand rapt in awe, is as good as dead: his eyes are closed.*
> **Albert Einstein**

My first experience with Death as a young Girl

As a young girl growing up in rural Ireland the experience of death eluded me. I was too busy running through the fields and playing with my friends to stop and notice death. There was an old woman in the village called Anne who babysat us every now and then. She lived in a tiny stone cottage down the road from my home. She was a unique and most loving character. Her cottage had no electricity, no running water, no heating, no indoor toilet, and no television. Despite all she lacked she was always happy and always singing. She loved her Mills & Boon books which she read by the light gleaned from a paraffin lamp. To visit her in her humble abode was like having received a rite of passage into her sacred temple. Although she was poor she always managed to have little treats put aside for my visits. Then one day Anne died. This was the first time I heard of death. In my mind as a child, it was the most incredible news. She was gone and would never come back. As a child I was heartbroken and no one could tell me where she was gone. My parents said she was gone to heaven, but it seemed like a fairytale when pitted against her disappearing. I could not believe it. Death came out of nowhere and snatched her from me. What impacted me most was how silently death came without any warning and took her from us. I can honestly say that the day Anne died was the first day I lost the innocence of my childhood to the grimness of death. As a child, Anne was a significant loss in my life and yet no one sat me down to ask, *"How are you feeling?"* In those days it was felt that children did not grieve because they were too young to understand. I know it is impossible to protect a child from the pain of loss, but it is fundamental to help a child feel safe and secure when dealing with loss. Encouraging a child to express their feelings can help build healthy skills that will serve them in dealing with future losses.

Helping Children Navigate the emotions of Grief

*I did not know what to say to him. I felt awkward and blundering.
I did not know how I could reach him, where I could overtake him
and go hand-in-hand with him once more. It is such a secret place,
the land of tears.*
Antoine de Saint-Exupéry, *The Little Prince*

The above-mentioned passage by the author expresses how difficult it was for the pilot to reach the Little Prince in his sadness in his land of tears. Many adults experience similar difficulties when trying to reach the world of a child after the loss of someone significant in their life. The adult mind often wants to protect the child from feeling the pain of loss. In doing so the child can feel disconnected and removed from the process. In the long-term overprotection can be counterproductive and will manifest later as the child moves through life and experiences other losses in adulthood. The moral and secret behind the story of the Little Prince is that "life is meaningful when it is filled with caring relationships."

It is only with the heart that one can see rightly: What is essential is Invisible to the eye – you become responsible forever, for what you have tamed.
Antoine de Saint-Exupéry, *The Little Prince*

The Story of Valerie: the child who carried her childhood grief into adulthood

Such was the story of one of my participants who attended my workshop on life after death. Valerie was 11 years old when her mother died. Her father sat her on his lap and explained that, *"Mammy died this morning."* But in the midst of her crying her father got up, walked away, went into the bedroom and shut the door behind him. Her mother was never mentioned again, and she was not allowed to attend her funeral. One day after Valerie came home from school she noticed all the photographs of her mother were gone. She ran into her mother's room, it was empty. Her dressing table that once hosted all her lovely perfumes, makeup and jewelry was bare. The emptiness of the room scared her as the reality of her mother's absence became an intense reality. In her distraught state Valerie looked around for some sign that she existed. Then she spotted her mother's photo album tucked away in the back of the wardrobe. She remembered helping her mother put some of the photographs into the album while her mother's gentle voice told a story as each photograph was set neatly in its place. Valerie carried the album into her bedroom and hid it under her bed. No one ever missed it or asked about it from that day onwards. She kept the album throughout her childhood and into her adult life. During the course of the workshop Valerie realized that the album was the only remaining connection she had to her mother, especially as her father chose to remain in a state of silence whenever she mentioned her mother. In essence, the album held the memories which in turn helped her grieve. It helped her remember all the lovely things she had shared with her mother which gave her a solid connection. Although Valerie was left without a platform for healing her loss, she created her own.

Valerie was 31 when she attended my workshop; she specialized as an intensive care nurse. It was while attending this workshop that she twenty years later came to terms with healing her childhood grief. Through a sacred guided meditation Valerie was spiritually reunited with her mother in the *Garden of Remembrance*. In this place they looked through the old photo album and reminisced on times they shared and the lost time they wished they had. Before Valerie left the sacred garden her mother imparted a very profound message to her. Afterwards Valerie shared with the group how the 11-year-old child climbed the staircase to heaven, but to her inexpressible joy the 31-year-old adult came down. The floodgates opened as twenty years of tears were released and brought forward for healing. Valerie left the workshop that day with a zest for life and a thirst for living her own life. For years she lived in the shadows of her grief which held her hostage from achieving her own goals and dreams. She finally had permission to live again. Always remember talking to a child about death or an impending death will not harm them. It will open a healthy dialogue where truth, honesty and trust can shape the child's perception of loss which will affect how they grieve in future losses. It's important for the adult to show the child ways to honor the memory of a loved one, rather than leave it as an unsolved mystery as it was in Valerie's case. (The meditation on climbing the staircase to heaven is included at the end of the book, Meditation: Loved One's A Whisper Away.)

Children are old enough to Grieve if they are old enough to Love: They are the "Forgotten Grievers."
Dr. Elisabeth Kübler-Ross

I was involved in facilitating the Rainbows Program for children of bereaved, separated and divorced families. From years of intense observation it was quite obvious that how the child responds emotionally to death and loss will have been predetermined by what they have learned as a child. In my experience it was often the case that parents felt the need to cover up or communicate only part of the truth in order to protect their children. However, honest and truthful communication shared in a loving and caring way will always help a child deal with the trauma and shock of loss. The key is to share the truth gradually, keeping in mind the age of the child together with their level of understanding. Very often children do not have the resources to verbalize their emotions or feelings through words. When this happens the child may become withdrawn or exhibit behaviors that are totally out of character with that of the child. In these situations it is best to seek the help of a professional grief counselor that specializes in child grief therapy. Art and clay therapies are an amazing platform that allows children to express their grief through nonverbal mediums. By using these therapeutic tools children can express their feelings through creative drawings or imagery icons. These act as a means of communication that allows the child to communicate in a way that doesn't require words. It gives permission to express freely what's on the child's mind and in its heart. To ask a child to draw *"how they are feeling"* can result in a mind-blowing story of pain, fear and sadness. The pictures tell the story, the images portray the missing pieces, the colors depict the mood, the resolution on the page highlights the anger and frustration that is locked within screaming to get out. With time and patience these interventions can help a parent to connect with their child and help form a deeper insight into their emotional world.

Techniques to Facilitate Children through the Grieving Process

The caterpillar dies so the butterfly could be born. And, yet the caterpillar lives in the butterfly and they are but one. So when I die, it will be that I have been transformed from the caterpillar of earth to the butterfly of the universe.
John Harricharan

As mentioned earlier it is always wise to prepare a child for the impending death. Chances are the child has already sensed and knows that something is wrong as a cloud of mystery punctuates the many whisperings. Depending on the age of the child it is always good to give an analogy. For example, *"Mammy is in a coma right now similar to a caterpillar in a cocoon. She can still hear everything you say, but she can no longer respond or talk to you."* At this stage to relate the story of the caterpillar to a child can be very empowering and positive. Explain to the child that the caterpillar at the right time will leave its cocoon and emerge into a new form of life or rebirth as a beautiful butterfly. This in turn can be likened to the person about to transition, as they shed their physical body to take on a new life form or a new resurrection of the soul in another plane of existence or in a place called heaven. Leading up to an impending death it is healthy to encourage the child/children to partake in the following rituals:

- Encourage the child to sit on the bed of the person about to transition (if appropriate).
- Encourage the child to give hugs and cuddles to the person – even if in a coma.
- Encourage the child to sing songs or tell stories of normal happenings.
- Encourage the child to gently touch the person – this normalizes the situation.
- Encourage the child to talk freely – using words of love and laughter.
- Encourage the child to play the person's favorite music.
- Encourage the child to hold hands and interlink – this stabilizes the connection.
- Encourage the child (when the time is right) to say goodbye – I love you.

Much of the work I have done with children following the death of a loved one proves very therapeutic when the child feels involved in or part of the process. I always encourage the child to write a letter or draw a picture and place it with their loved one. This gives the child the opportunity to say what is in their heart or say the things they wished they had said but didn't get the chance. This can become part of the child's ritual by placing the items in the coffin with their loved one. The child who was encouraged to be part of the dying/grieving process will have vivid recall in adulthood of what they drew and what they wrote in their letter. The child who is part of the process grows up with healthier attitudes and more realistic coping skills in dealing with grief and loss.

How to help Children continue a positive connection with a Loved One

The death of a parent or loved one can be a very traumatic event in the life of a child. Following the passing of a loved one the child needs to know that their loved one still loves them and wishes to continue to be part of the child's life. In general children have an advantage over many adults simply because children are naturally open and receptive to multidimensional energies and very often possess intuitive gifts and abilities. Therefore it is not unusual for children who are encouraged to develop their psychic gifts to have the ability to connect with their loved one in spirit. I would like to share with you some of the statements that parents/carers have heard in the aftermath of a death:

> *"Mammy was with me last night, she sat on top of my bed and told me not to be afraid, she wouldn't let anything bad happen to me."*
>
> *"Granddad came to me last night, I wasn't afraid of him, he said he would be at the match on Saturday and help me score a goal."*
>
> *"I saw Kelley in a bright light at the bottom of my bed."*
>
> *"Nana was in my room last night and she sang to me, she looked like an angel."*
>
> *"Oscar helped me finish my jigsaw, I didn't finish it on my own."*
>
> *"Daddy touched my hair and called me princess and said he'd mind me."*

Children sense their loved one's presence and it is important that adults do not dismiss or make little of what the child may be experiencing. No matter what the perception of the adult is, and from personal experiences, it is very much advised to encourage the child to continue to talk about the experiences. Remember children are very intuitive and highly sensitive, they take in a lot more than the spoken word. Without doubt, more and more children have the ability to communicate with the unseen realms of heaven and their loved ones who reside there. Children sense the loving energy of their loved one around them and that is why they are not afraid, because it is familiar and known to them. The best response to a child's report of communicating

with their mother/father would be, *"tell me about it,"* or *"that's wonderful,"* or *"let's sit and chat about that."* These open-ended sentences allow the child to feel safe in their disclosure and it allows for a spontaneous conversation to take place. The worst response from an adult to a child that revealed, *"Mammy came and sat on my bed last night,"* would be, *"That is ridiculous,"* or *"Shut up and don't ever say anything like that again,"* or *"Don't let anyone hear you say that,"* or *"That's nonsense, go to your room right now."* The attitude between these two very different responses will determine how the child will cope with the loss in a healthy or non-healthy way. The responsible adult will remind the child that their loved one is always there, watching over them and will be with them throughout all the significant milestones of their life.

Healthy Techniques to help Children Express their Grief

The following are a number of simple techniques that can be used to facilitate the grieving process in children. Integrating the loss through using these will support children in a more holistic and therapeutic manner.

Create a Sacred Place

Select an area in the child's home that will be a special place for the child to go when they are feeling sad or lonely. My advice is to choose a corner of a room that is bright, spacious and boasts lots of energy. With the child's participation allow them to choose where to place a small table and chair in that space. Allow the child to select one or more favorite photographs of their loved one and display them on the table or wall. If it is the child's wish to place a piece of clothing or garment belonging to their loved one on the chair, allow the child to do so, as this garment will still hold their loved one's energy and scent. The child may wish to decorate the table with garden flowers or place other items on the table that the child associates with their loved one. Explain to the child that this is their sacred place to go to at any time when they are sad or when they wish to be close to their loved one. This becomes the child's hideout – while the child is still observed and remains in full view of the caring adult.

Create a Direct Telephone Line

Depending on the age of the child create a special call center in some area of the child's home. Invest in an inexpensive telephone that is colorful and very different to any other phones in the house. Place this in a designated place selected by the child. The phone is a very effective tool to help the child feel connected to their loved one. Tell the child that this is their special telephone just for talking to Mammy/Daddy. Tell them when they are feeling sad all they have to do is lift their special telephone and say, "Hello Mammy/Daddy, I just want to talk to you and tell you that I miss you." The child will have a strong awareness that their loved one is on the other end of the telephone and can hear them perfectly. Children have not been taught that such things are impossible and will be instinctively open and receptive to spirit transmissions. However, it is important to note that the adults in the child's life should never dismiss or discourage the child's reports of hearing, seeing or having communication from their loved one.

Create Time for Letter Writing

Letter writing is very beneficial during the grieving process for the child. It can be a very powerful tool in that it creates an easy outlet for the child to express their thoughts and feelings that otherwise they would not feel comfortable sharing with someone else. It's important to reassure the child that whatever they write in their letter their loved one will never be angry or upset with them. Reassure the child that it's okay to write everything that's on their minds and how they are feeling.

Encourage the child to write from the heart. This will help bring negative emotional energies to the surface, for example sadness, loneliness, frustration, anger, fear, guilt, blame, and prevent them being suppressed. If any of these emotions are ignored they can cause serious emotional issues for the child that often continue into adulthood.

Create a Family Hour

One of the most valuable assets to a grieving family is the creation of a family hour. This is where the family in the aftermath of a loss will set aside on a weekly basis a time for family gatherings. This method facilitates family members to discuss their feelings and any fears they may need answers to about the future. At this point the togetherness of the family unit can empower vulnerable children to feel loved and cared for by other caring adults. For the adult leading the family hour, it is important to ask, *"What do you think Mammy/Daddy would say about that?"* This open-ended statement encourages the child to talk freely keeping healthy memories of their loved one alive. It is important to encourage the child to have ongoing discussions about their loved one during and after family hour. Often, something may arise resulting from the family hour for the child and it is important for the child to know they can still talk even after family hour is over. As I mentioned children have a natural awareness of their loved one's presence and must be acknowledged and respected by the adult.

Create an Arts & Crafts Activity Session

The use of arts and crafts is one of the many tools that provide a platform for children experiencing grief. These therapeutic activities play a powerful role in providing a safe format where children can share their feelings and begin the healing process. The following are a few examples of arts and crafts projects that can facilitate children to express their grief.

Create a Memory Box

A memory box will allow the child to create a special collection of significant items that reminds the child of the treasured memories they shared with their loved one. Whatever the child places in the memory box is relevant to them. The memory box can become a treasure trove of magic, almost like an Aladdin's cave containing photographs, little trinkets, buttons, toys, ticket stubs, jewelry, ribbons and lots more. When the child is missing their loved one the most, the memory box can open the child's mind to the love and memories that is contained in every item with each and every touch.

Create a Balloon Releasing Ceremony

A balloon releasing ceremony can be performed at any time in memory of a loved one. Having balloons released into the skies can allow the grieving child to visualize messages of love being sent to their loved one in the heavens. This process can help alleviate any guilt the child may be feeling that was left unsaid to the loved one. A balloon ceremony is very effective when marking occasions like anniversaries, birthdays, Mother's Day/Father's Day, Christmas, other holidays or at any stage that the child wishes to mark an occasion to make it special.

I believe the most valuable support any adult can possibly offer to a grieving child is to be present; just be there, no need to fill the empty silences with words. You can let the child know that it is okay to talk or not to talk about it. But that you will be there whenever they are ready. There is nothing more powerful for the grieving child than knowing they are loved and supported beyond their valley of tears.

What we once enjoyed and deeply loved, we can never lose. For all that we love deeply becomes part of us.
Helen Keller

Before concluding this section on children it is important to be aware that some children and in particular younger children are able to perceive more than what adults perceive as normal or real. These children are born with psychic abilities and are tuned in to higher frequencies that are otherwise lost to the adult conditioned mind. I firmly believe that more and more children are coming on earth now with extraordinary gifts which allow them to communicate with the invisible realms of heaven. Pay attention when your child suddenly goes silent and stares at a particular corner of a room. Watch out for signs when your child is playing and you hear laughter and chat coming from the playroom. Chances are if you ask the child, *"Who are you talking to or who are you playing with?"* you will hear, *"I am playing with my friend."* If you ask the child to describe their friend, you will be given a detailed description of another person, who is visible to the child, but invisible to the adult. For the child the veil between the two worlds is very thin which in turn allows their consciousness to inter-penetrate and fluctuate quite normally between the two worlds. Young children are not subjected to cultural norms or adult programming; therefore they remain uncontaminated vessels of pure light. The following is a true and genuine story of a young girl who can remember visions of heaven since she was a baby.

Young Akiane remembers visits of Jesus while she was in the cradle

One such child is Akiane Kramarik, a young artist whose paintings are inspired by visions of God. Akiane was born in July 1994, Illinois. Her mother was Lithuanian and father was an atheist. They lived in a shack, had no running water and barely any furniture. They were poor and basic essentials like food and clothing were sparse. Akiane the young prodigy says that she met God while in her cradle as a baby. She said God began showing her visions of heaven from the age of four years. She believes that God gives her the visions and then helps her to paint them so that her artwork will teach others. She describes God as a ball of light who bestows upon her a rite of passage into the other world. At the age of eight years, Akiane's desire to paint the face of Jesus consumed her every waking moment. After months of relentless hours of painting, getting up at 4am each morning, the renowned portrait titled *Prince of Peace* was birthed. This portrait remains one of the most coveted *"Jesus Christ"* paintings in the world. Akiane believes that she has been chosen by God for one reason and one reason only: "to help others." Akiane's masterful artworks have to be seen in order to believe that God is the credible divine source of her heavenly inspirations. (To view her miraculous work you can visit her official website: www.akiane.com.)

Poem: *Loss of a Child*

And a woman who held a babe against her bosom said, "Speak to us of Children." And he said: "Your children are not your children.

They are the sons and daughters of Life's longings for itself. They came through you but not from you. And though they are with you yet they belong not to you.

You may give them your love but not your thoughts, for they have their own thoughts.

You may house their bodies but not their souls, for their souls dwell in the house of tomorrow, which you cannot visit, not even in your dreams.

You may strive to be like them, but seek not to make them like you, for life goes not backward nor tarries with yesterday.

You are the bows from which your children as living arrows are sent forth. The Archer sees the mark upon the path of the Infinite, and he bends you with his might that his arrows may go swift and far.

Let your bending in the Archer's hand be for gladness: For even

as He loves the arrow that flies, so He loves the bow that is stable."
Kahlil Gibran

Zen Buddhist story on Sharing the Sorrow

Soyen Shaku, the abbot, each morning took a walk accompanied by his companion from the monastery to the nearby town. One day, as he passed a house, he heard a great cry from within it. Stopping to inquire, he asked the inhabitants, "Why are you all wailing so?" They said, "Our child has died and we are grieving." The abbot without hesitation sat down with the family and started crying and wailing himself. As they were returning to the monastery, the abbot's companion asked, "Master, is this family known to you?" "No," the abbot answered. "Why then, Master, did you cry?" The abbot said simply, "So that I may share in their sorrow."
The inspirational book *As You Grieve*

Burial Rituals and Ceremonies

The above story is very symbolic of the rituals and ceremonies from my Irish heritage. I remember when somebody died the entire community would go into mourning with the grieving family. In those times the *"merry wake"* was a way of honoring the deceased and was a respected and followed tradition in the majority of the country. The *"merry wake"* was a catalyst for family, friends and neighbors to mourn in public. It was a mixture of celebration and mourning rubbing shoulder to shoulder in honoring the dead. There was room to reminisce, to laugh, to cry, to share stories, or just be a silent witness. There was no pressure to perform or be anything other than how you were. This mourning tradition facilitated the public expression of grief and provided support for the bereaved. The death of a person was a public ritual. It involved the whole community fusing together in taking on specific tasks. Neighbors moved into the house, food was prepared, music was arranged, while at the same time every person that came through the door to pay their respects was as the cliché goes *"fed and watered."* All-night vigils were maintained around the deceased until the time of burial. Grief was expressed in an unrestrained and healthy way that was cathartic and communally shared.

Sadly, this is very much in contrast with the modern emphasis on controlling one's emotions and keeping grief private. I know many people who during funerals hold back their tears in order to feel in control. There is no shame in shedding tears; in fact it brings integrity to the deep loss that is personally yours. In various countries the outpouring of emotions is not only required but performed ceremonially in the form of ritualized wailing and weeping. The ancient Celts coined this tradition as the *"death wail"* which still exists in various indigenous areas today, such as Australia, South America, Africa and Asia. This ritual allowed family members to cry their grief out loud thus enabling the pain to find an escape route from the body. In similar fashion, the Irish and Scottish tradition of *"keening"* was a central part of the mourning process. If the family were unable to cry the *"keeners"* stepped in. They were professional female mourners who would wail and cry out loud to mourn and honor the dead. These expressions of sorrow were a powerful way to give voice to the reality of the individual loss and the impact shared within the wider community. It is my belief that these mourning traditions facilitated the separation of the deceased from the world of the living while at the same time symbolized the transition of the loved one to the afterlife. These traditions gave testimony to the life of the deceased by allowing the outward expression of grief in a way that is/was consistent with its cultural values and beliefs.

Similar to the monk in the above passage, it is important to share in people's sorrow during times of great loss and sadness. Personally, I find it disheartening that these rituals and customs are less common especially in the larger cities. In many places in Ireland the *"merry wake"* is a dying ritual of the past while the funeral homes gain prominence for the future. One of the saddest things I hear over the radio or written in the newspaper is *"house private."* While this is becoming the norm many people decide to stay away from the bereaved family, feeling the family have enough to deal with and do not wish to be disturbed. In these circumstances it is difficult to grieve in a balanced way as grieving is done in isolation of others.

With modern embalming techniques time to hold onto a loved one for a few days longer is extended and this has led to somewhat of a revival of the *"merry wake"* albeit in a more muted form. Families are much happier to bring their loved one back home for a few nights before the burial/cremation day. This ritual brings comfort to the family, it allows time to sit, talk, cry, touch and gaze upon their loved one. It allows time for family, friends and neighbors to find an intimate space to grieve collectively. Finally, as the loved one leaves home for the last time, there is a sense of completion having done the best for your loved one. In time this ritual will also bring a sense of meaning and closure to the bereaved.

Unable are the Loved to die. For Love is Immortality.
Emily Dickinson

How you lay your loved one to rest will depend on many factors including what traditions and belief system your loved one held sacred. There are various ways to give your loved one the send-off they deserve. Chances are your deceased loved one will have discussed this with a family member, making it easier to carry out their final wishes. In Ireland, the funeral ritual remains the most popular and traditional. The ceremony is rich in history and steeped in symbolism which helps the bereaved acknowledge the reality of death. The funeral provides a gathering place for people to show their solidarity with the bereaved. Demonstrations of affection like a hug, an embrace, a touch, a handshake all are worthy substitutes when words are inadequate. Remember your physical presence is the most valuable show of support for the living exposing the fact that they are not alone in their grief.

If you know someone who is recently bereaved, lift the phone and give them a call. Even if they don't answer leave a message saying that you are there for them whenever they are ready to talk. If you are worried about someone who has gone into hibernation take courage and ring the doorbell. Call their name through the letter box if you have to; just say you are checking in to see if they are okay then you can go away once you have communicated with them. The best act of kindness is to leave a small food parcel outside someone's door with a little note saying, *"I'm thinking of you."* I remember when my brother passed away, the amount of delicious food that was left on my doorstep will never be forgotten, it was so appreciated. No one rang the doorbell or shouted through the letter box, just a caring friend or neighbor not wishing to impose but letting me know I was loved and cherished and that I was not alone. As rituals and traditions fade away it is now more important than ever to make time to share in the sorrow of another demonstrating that they are loved and supported throughout their grieving journey.

When I was born and saw the light I was no stranger in this world. Something inscrutable, shapeless and without words appeared in the form of my mother. So when I die, the same unknown will appear again as ever known to me, and because I love this life, I will love death as well.
Rabindranath Tagore

A Wife's Wonderful Humor in the face of Husband's final act of Malice

The old Irish cliché *"you made your bed, you must lay on it"* was responsible for many couples living in abject misery. The ramifications from a God-fearing Church for anyone who would leave a marriage was deemed a punishable offense and as a consequence many chose to remain in a loveless marriage. In such circumstances when a spouse died it was liberation of sorts even a blessing as expressed in the following story "Life after Loss."

Molly suffered forty years of matrimonial disharmony, tethered to a man who gave her a ring, sired her children and then retired into unconcerned bachelorhood. Eventually, he did the decent thing, he died. But he planted a codicil in his will to the effect that he wanted to be cremated and have his ashes scattered on the Ganges, the holy river in India. Even the most charitable observers saw it for what it was, his final act of malice, intended to deprive Molly of the paltry comfort of his insurance. Her neighbors gathered round to support her, and eventually, one of them plucked up the courage to ask: "Molly, how will you manage the ashes?" "Arrah, girl," she replied with newfound confidence, "I'll flush them down the toilet and he can make his own bloody way to the Ganges."
Christy Kenneally

Conversely, relationships that are destroyed by hurt and pain often feel free when the death of a spouse occurs. In cases similar to these, it is important that a process of forgiveness is undertaken by the surviving spouse in order for healing to take place. See the Powerful Forgiveness Exercise, on page 162.

Learning to Identify the Stages and Phases of Grief

You are not going Mad – You are Grieving. The pain felt after the loss of a loved one is a normal part of the grieving process. Please, allow yourself time and space to feel the pain and loss; it is not physically, nor spiritually healthy to deny or suppress these feelings. If somewhere along life's journey your love for someone got lost or tainted, by arguments, disrespect or control, remember where your loved one now resides, there are no judgments, only pure unconditional love. Sometimes the life of a loved one can appear all too short. In truth nobody dies before their time. No matter what way your loved one's life ended, be it accident, suicide, illness, war, natural disaster, murder, fire or drowning, the soul chooses its exit point. This is a very hard lesson for families especially if the person was young.

The renowned Elisabeth Kübler-Ross (1969) introduced a theory known as the *"five stages of grief."* Over time other theorists, Bowlby, Parkes, Stroebe & Schut, modified this framework to adapt to other life challenges including the loss of a loved one. This framework is not an exact science nor does it follow a precise order or timeline. The stages identified include: denial, anger, bargaining, depression and acceptance. There is no definitive time as to how long you dwell on any one stage over the other. All stages are of personal significance and often become blended together creating a web of confusion where there are no answers, no logic, only intense pain. You may experience all kinds of unexpected emotions from disbelief, numbness, shock, anger, betrayal, guilt and deep sadness. All of these emotions are natural responses to your loss.

Denial

Denial prevents you from becoming completely overwhelmed with grief. Right now you may feel that life makes no sense and has lost its meaning. The magnitude of it all is too much for your body to cope with. You are afraid if you allow all your feelings to come to the surface at once that you will never feel normal again. You are in a state of shock and life as you once knew it has changed forever. Your world has become empty and meaningless. Your world has been ripped apart and you wonder how you will cope and go on. You cannot believe why this has happened to you. You may have many questions with few answers. You may say, *"I am a good person, I have never done anyone wrong, why me?"* Right now, there are no right or wrong answers. Be patient, loving and kind with the chaotic feelings that are paralyzing your body. Denial is the safety net that shields you from the full reality of your loss. Give yourself time to come to terms with the emptiness you are feeling. As denial fades the impact of your loss gradually becomes your reality. When this happens be patient and gentle with yourself.

Affirmation: *Today I acknowledge my pain and the mystery of death before me. I create a loving relationship with myself and those around me. I let go of the relentless torture of myself and find peace in this now moment. I bless myself completely.*

Anger

Your anger is a natural reaction to the loss of your loved one. You protest about life being so unfair as death becomes an unwelcome stranger to your door. Anger is your friend and companion giving you temporary refuge from the enormity of your loss. It is important to remember that the anger you are feeling only raises its ugly head when you feel safe enough to survive the pain. Try not to suppress the anger you are feeling. Over time suppressed anger turns to resentment leading to a buildup of toxic chemicals which eventually attack the body's defense mechanisms causing disease within the body. Release all the feelings you harbor of guilt, shame or blame which are haunting your days and nights. If you could change things you would in a heartbeat, but this cannot be so. You feel angry with the world and angry that you are left alone and abandoned in this great ocean of life without a lifejacket. Anger becomes the mask you can hide your frustration behind. Anger can extend to the medical and care team, family members, religion, even God gets a bashing. Assuming God is the miracle worker, why did he not think it worthwhile to save my loved one? You feel let down by everyone and feel no one cares. The loneliness you feel leaves a great big gaping hole in your heart that nothing can ever fill. Try and find healthy ways to externalize your anger, digging the garden, walk by the sea, walk in nature, take up yoga or talk to a trusted friend. It is okay to feel anger as this allows you to feel the rawness of your pain. In time when anger subsides you will honor the memory of your loved one by creating a positive attitude of gratitude for life.

Affirmation: *I ask God to take my hand this day to give me courage and strength to live through another day. Catch me as I fall, hold me when I cry, let me feel your love, hear your whispers in my ear and as night fades I ask God to grant me restful sleep from all anger as serenity and peace enfold my heart.*

Bargaining

During the bargaining stage you may find yourself creating a lot of *"what if"* and *"if only"* statements. You long for the life you once knew to return again. If only you could rewind the clock things would be different. If you hadn't been so busy with life, you may have noticed your loved one getting weaker, or if you had insisted on her/him attending the doctor sooner, or if you had stopped him/her from driving the car that day, the accident may never have happened. Stop punishing yourself; none of this was your fault and was beyond your control. You may bargain with God to take the pain and sadness away. You may promise to be a better person, kinder to strangers, rescue an animal, carry out random acts of kindness, all in the hope of changing the unchangeable. Be aware that negotiating with God or whoever you believe in is your way of giving your body the time it needs to heal and adjust after your loss. This kind of bargaining is helping you keep your suffering at a distance. It also shields you from the heartbreak of the true reality. Out of desperation you may even bargain that someday you will see your loved one again in heaven.

Affirmation: *Everywhere I go, I feel your presence, every breath I take, I know you are there, every tear I shed you kiss it dry, every sleepless night, you are by my side. Safely in my heart you will always be.*

Depression

Feeling depressed is a natural reaction to the loss of a loved one. You may feel like hiding or withdrawing from everyone even life itself. Your grief and sense of depression is keeping you safe and protected. Shutting down your emotions is a way of helping you to adjust to something you cannot handle. If your sadness is deep seated and you feel stuck with no aspirations for your future, please seek the support of a professional who will work with you on your healing journey. Sometimes with the best will in the world some temporary chemical intervention may be required. This may be for a brief period of time whereby your medical doctor may prescribe a course of antidepressants to lift your mood. (This is totally a personal choice.) Alternatively, a trip to your local health shop will also give you the necessary advice on herbal and natural remedies that are equally as beneficial. Try and adopt a healthy attitude towards relaxing the mind through the practice of meditation and mindfulness. In the stillness you will learn to calm your mind and listen to the voice of wisdom. By embracing such practices you will find inner peace through the breath rather than listening to the ranting and raging of a busy mind. You will truly benefit from meditation, and by doing so, when your mind is peaceful, your loved one will be able to communicate with you from beyond the veil. This can happen through signs, symbols, synchronicities mentioned earlier (After Death Communication, page 78). Acknowledge your feelings and make friends with them. Feelings are not meant to be depressed, they are meant to be expressed.

Affirmation: *I am with you always, in the quiet of the night I watch over you while you are sleeping, in the breaking of the morning I go before you to light up your day. I am your constant companion and heavenly friend. You are never alone as I am with you always. There is no separation, only pure love.*

Acceptance

Acceptance is not necessarily a transformative or uplifting stage of grief. However, it does mean that you are acknowledging the loss and coming to terms with new ways of coping and living with the past. At this stage you are acknowledging that life as you knew it has changed forever and you realize that holding onto the pain is serving no purpose only keeping you stuck in an emotional prison. You understand your loved one can never be replaced, but you move and grow into your new reality. Be gentle with yourself as you pursue new ways of living again, for example, a new relationship, new home, new career or new car. Accept the hand of friendship that is extended to you. Accept the fact that no one understands how broken you truly are, even though they try. By allowing these new energies to occur you are embracing change without feeling you are dishonoring your loved one. Finally, when the good days outnumber the bad days life takes on a whole new meaning again.

Affirmation: *May all negative thoughts, feelings and emotions be transmuted and transformed into the greatness and presence of a loving God. May those I love be safe and protected always in a world of unpredictability. With God's grace I come to a place of understanding, the rhythm of life, the seasons of birth, death, and rebirth and the journey of my soul. From this day forward I shall plant the seeds of love wherever I go, love, peace and harmony.*

Descriptions of other types of Grief and Loss

To experience grief and loss is an inevitable part of the human existence. There are many reasons which activate grief beyond the loss of a loved one. Other losses to mention include loss of marriage, loss of career, loss of home, loss of relationship, loss of ex-spouse, loss of family pet, loss of a treasured friend, loss of mental agility, loss of independence, loss of financial security and loss through miscarriage. The manner in which you grieve depends on what kind of loss you have suffered and how significant the loss is to you personally. The following are descriptions of different types of grief although there are myriad other types, but these I find are the most common.

Anticipatory Grief

For some months before my mother died there was a sense of foreboding around her home. As her health deteriorated her world became more hushed by the lack of her ability to converse. It was a sad time made even more difficult by the fact that we as a family were anticipating our own grief while she was still physically with us. What would life be like without her and what way would we deal with the grief individually and collectively as a family when the time came? However, anticipating her death allowed each member of the family to spend meaningful and quality time with her. This gave rise to finding a sense of closure and peace.

Normal Grief

I find this one a bit funny – in the sense that there is nothing normal about grief. Normal grief includes the same powerless feelings of shock and disbelief with the loss of a loved one. The one common difference is that the person can still function and continue with basic daily activities where work and family are concerned. Although normal grief is still very painful, many people are able to cope with their loss and even grow from the experience.

Delayed Grief

I can certainly identify with this concept. My father died very suddenly, without warning and without any time to say "goodbye." At that time I did not cry, I showed no emotions whatsoever. The shock and deep sadness numbed me. Three years later when I was attending the funeral of my beautiful friend the floodgates burst open. I was inconsolable – I sobbed my heart out until there were no more tears left. It took another significant loss for me to fully experience the enormity of my father's death and come to terms with that delayed loss years later.

Complicated Grief

One of my clients lost her husband in a car accident. She was overwhelmed with grief. She was constantly thinking about his death, the lost opportunities to try and save their marriage. Her obsession with his death was beginning to develop into a mental issue. While delving deeper into her situation I discovered the real reason for her catastrophizing. She had been having an affair for over two years. The shame and guilt were complicating her grief to the extent she was nearing a nervous breakdown. I put her in touch with a psychologist who over time helped her find meaning and purpose in her life again.

Disenfranchised Grief

Disenfranchised grief is grief that is judged or minimized where the importance of the loss is not recognized as significant. This can include the loss of mental ability through dementia, loss of a body part, loss through miscarriage, loss of a pet, loss of someone you admire. For example, when Lady Diana died the outpour of grief was felt throughout the entire world. Yet there were some who, because they did not know her personally, felt all the grieving and tears were unnecessary. This thinking was due to the fact that while the world mourned her death few people actually knew her intimately, so why get caught up in shedding tears for someone you don't even know or have ever met.

Ambiguous Grief

Ambiguous grief is where the body of the loved one has never been found.

This type of grief is one of the most challenging and difficult to deal with. Many loved ones have been lost through air disasters, drowning at sea, tsunamis, fires, earthquakes, wars, abductions where no physical body can be found. This is a cruel blow to families; their world stops as grief becomes frozen in time. They forever wait and hope – maybe someday the body of their loved one will be returned to them. Hu Xianqun, the wife of a passenger on Flight 370 (the Malaysian plane which disappeared over the Indian Ocean in 2014), referenced an ancient old Chinese proverb: *"If a person is alive, we need to see him as proof. If a person is dead, we need to see the body. We relatives haven't seen anything yet, so how can we give up hope?"* With this type of grief families find themselves in a state of limbo where closure is never truly reached.

Exercise: Identifying the Five Stages of Grief on your Healing Journey

The following exercise will help you Identify the Stages of Grief and where you may presently be on your Grieving/Healing Journey. I encourage you to find a quiet space where you cannot be disturbed. Give yourself permission to sit and be with your emotions/thoughts and feelings. If it is your preference you may wish to play some gentle music in the background.

The following questions are used here as a catalyst to assist you in acknowledging where you are in your grief/healing Journey. Please be as honest and open with yourself as possible. Circle what is appropriate and write in the space provided.

How long is it since the loss of your Loved One?

Can you name other losses you have experienced & how they affected you?

Where do you see yourself now in the grieving process – Anger / Denial / Bargaining / Depression / Acceptance? Discuss how you feel about any of these stages.

List the major changes / events that have taken place in your life since your loss, i.e. birthdays / weddings / anniversaries / christenings / Christmas / Mother's Day / Father's Day.

Do you have any feelings of Regret / Guilt / Secrets weighing heavily on your mind at this time? Are they realistic or unrealistic? Explain why.

Have you tried to "Move On" too quickly without giving time and space to the pain of your loss?

Have you experienced a "Connection" with your loved one since they passed through signs / dreams / visitations / a feeling of presence?

After completing the exercise, allow yourself time to absorb the answers you have written. Be gentle with yourself and know that this process is part of the healing you are embracing right now. In time you may wish to revisit these questions and rewrite the answers. This process is very therapeutic as you find your answers/attitudes will have changed from your original answers.

Grieving the Loss of a Child: Broken Heart Syndrome

Over many years of running workshops on bereavement and loss I have to say the loss of a child is one of the most devastating of all losses. There are no words adequate enough to describe this unfortunate tragedy. With the loss of a child the guilt can be complicated by the feelings of injustice, *"this should never have happened."* During the early stages of grief many parents speak of an excruciating pain in their heart. Some people have ended up at hospital emergency departments thinking their hearts were about to bust or that a heart attack was imminent. These life-threatening symptoms mimic those of a heart attack, shortness of breath, feeling of tightness with a stabbing pain in the chest area. But, when doctors delved deeper into these patients' symptoms, they found no signs of heart attack and more confusingly these patients' arteries were clear. Thankfully, research by Dr. Hikaru Sato (1990) accepts that this is a condition known as *"Takotsubo cardiomyopathy"* otherwise known as *"broken-heart syndrome."* This condition is attributed to many who experience sudden loss and in particular child loss. It is important to remember that bereaved parents can mourn the loss of a child at any age, be it miscarriage, stillbirth, four months, four years or forty years. When a parent loses a child they lose a part of themselves.

Peggy (one of my attendees) was searching for meaning after her daughter's death. She longed for understanding as to how her daughter's death could possibly have anything to do with the grand scheme of life. She had a great faith but now she felt betrayed by the God she trusted and believed in. Her faith was shattered. She had long believed that if she lived a good life, was a good person, made numerous contributions to worthy causes that life would turn out pretty good. The death of her daughter robbed her of that belief. In Sanskrit (an ancient language of India) the word *Vilomah* identifies the loss of a child as *"against the natural order of things."* By the very law of nature it is deemed unnatural for a parent to outlive their child; it feels like the ultimate betrayal in the cycle of life. Peggy's heart was broken and it would never be the same again. It took two years of intense emotional engagement with Peggy before she showed any sign of life manifesting in her body. I encouraged her to keep a grief/healing journal. I positively encouraged her to write letters to her daughter – outlining the ups and downs of her life without her. This proved very therapeutic, and by the end of the second anniversary Peggy felt her daughter was responding directly to her through her writing. Peggy believed her daughter had found a way to communicate with her mom through journaling and in doing so helped her find her way back to living again. Peggy hopes that some day she will have the courage to write an inspirational book on healing using the messages she received from her daughter in spirit. Without doubt, I fully endorse this healing modality. With an open heart and trust in your soul, spirit communication between the heavens and the earth is possible.

A wonderful book called *Our Children Forever: George Anderson's Messages from Children on the Other Side*, by Joel Martin and Patricia Romanowski, is a most profound book for any parent after the loss of a child.

The Most Inconsiderate Things you could say after the loss of a child

These types of statements minimize the emotions and loss the grieving parents feel.

"God would never give you a cross that you could not carry."
"He/she is in a better place now."
"Time is a great healer."

"You have an Angel watching over you from Heaven."
"Everything happens for a reason."
"You are young, you can still have more children."
"I could never be as strong as you are."
"It was part of God's plan."
"It doesn't get any easier."
"At least he/she didn't suffer, it was quick."
"Don't cry, you have to be strong now."
"How did he/she die?"

Examples of Helpful Statements that provide comfort and support

"I have no words, but I am here for you."
"Whenever you feel like talking – I am here to listen."
"It's okay to be angry with the world."
"I'll pick the kids up from school for you."
Put your arms around the person and hold them.
"You are in my thoughts and prayers."
"I know I can't take your pain away – but know I am only a call away."
"Tell me about the things he/she loved to do."

Rule of Thumb. If you can't think of anything to say – Say NOTHING at all.

Years ago while facilitating the Rainbows program (for children of bereaved and divorced parents) I stumbled upon this poem. It touched the very core of my being as it highlighted the courage it takes for a parent to say No to a child. It basically implies do not do for a child what he/she is capable of doing for itself.

Poem: *Love Till It Hurts*

"You don't love me." How many times have your kids laid that one on you? And how many times have you as parents resisted the urge to tell them how much? Someday, when your children are old enough to understand the logic that motivates a mother, you will tell them:

> *I loved you enough to bug you about where you were going, with whom, and what time you would get home.*
>
> *I loved you enough to insist you buy a bike with your own money that we could afford and you couldn't.*
>
> *I loved you enough to be silent and let you discover your handpicked friend was a creep. I loved you enough to make you return a bar of chocolate with a bite out of it to the grocery shop and say, "I stole this."*
>
> *I loved you enough to stand over you for two hours while you cleaned your bedroom, a job that would have taken me fifteen minutes. I loved you enough to say, "Yes you can go to Disney World on Mother's Day."*
>
> *I loved you enough to let you see anger, disappointment, disgust and tears in my eyes. I loved you enough to not make excuses for your lack of respect or your bad manners.*
>
> *I loved you enough to admit I was wrong and ask your forgiveness.*
>
> *I loved you enough to ignore what other mothers did or said. I loved you enough to let you stumble, fall, hurt and fail.*
>
> *I loved you enough to let you assume the responsibility for your own actions at six, ten, sixteen.*
>
> *I loved you enough to figure you would lie about the party being chaperoned, but forgave you for it … after I discovered I was right.*
>
> *I loved you enough to shove you off my lap, let go of your hand, be mute to your pleas, and insensitive to your demands so that you had to stand alone.*
>
> *I loved you enough to accept you for what you are, not what I*

wanted you to be.

But most of all, I loved you enough to say No when you hated me
for it. That was the hardest part of all.
Erma Bombeck

Out of your brokenness, know your child is not alone

The pain you are feeling is beyond words. Your world is turned
upside down and you feel you have nothing left to give. Your
heart is broken and you wish with all your heart to wake up
from this dreadful nightmare. It is unnatural for any parent
to lose a child, be it through illness, accident or otherwise.
You are not to blame, no one is. You did not have the power
to change the outcome of the circumstances. Your child's death
was preordained by its soul a long time ago. At the moment of
your child's passing, your child was not alone; many familiar
faces that he/she once knew created a bridge of rainbow light for
your child to step upon. They wrapped your child in the most
glorious blanket of light and placed your child lovingly within
the heart of God. Please take comfort in the knowing that your
child is being nurtured and loved by family members already
passed. Your child asks you to release your anger with God or
anyone else, trusting that he/she continues to grow and evolve
on the other side.

Heavenly Message from your Child

My lovely Mammy, Daddy and family, just to let you know I have
arrived okay. I am surrounded in the most beautiful light with God
and many radiant beings by my side. I am happy and much loved by
everyone. They call me God's Child. There are no words to describe
this special place; it is of the most unimaginable beauty I have ever
known. Other children are with me and we play in the garden of
bliss. Through the colors of the rainbow our mystical friends join
us and play. Please do not be sad as God holds my hand. Know that

I now live in this Promised Land. Be happy for the brief time we had together. Please know and try to understand that to grow up on earth was not part of my divine plan. Within the stars you will see my eyes, within the sunrise you will feel my smile. Touch your heart and know that I am there, I am right here beside you, only a whisper away.
Mariel

The above message came through while I was channeling a healing to a bereaved mother whose daughter had died at three years of age. With her permission I include it here in the hope it will bring as much comfort to you as it did to her.

Like a bird singing in the rain, let grateful memories survive in times of sorrow.
Robert Louis Stevenson

The Act of Suicide – Demystifying the Stigma

My father was a very enlightened soul. He was a wise man who understood the rhythm of nature and the cycles of life. He was never frightened by the wrath of God or hell's fire and damnation that was so often preached by the clergy of his time. On one particular occasion, I remember my father walking around an old graveyard and at various headstones would pause, bless himself and move on. I was curious when I saw him climb over the wall and disturb the ritual he had going on. I watched in silence as he stood and gazed upon a slab of stone that lay flat on the ground outside the graveyard wall. Eventually he blessed himself and climbed back over the wall. As we walked back to the car no words were spoken. The chatter had stopped and I knew my father was sad. I instantly went into his pocket for the cure. I pulled out his tobacco pipe and said, *"Here, Dada, take a blast out of that and it will put the life back into you."* As we sat on the ditch and composed ourselves he began to tell me that in

133

the past Ireland had a very archaic way of dealing with suicide. The Church frowned upon suicide and deemed it a crime, an unforgiveable sin, a passport to hell. He questioned why a Church dedicated to promoting a loving and compassionate God would deem a person unfit for burial in sacred ground if the person had ended his/her life through suicide. He elaborated further by saying that in those days the family of the suicide person was isolated and burdened with shame and guilt. The grieving family was left on their own to grieve. The neighbors and friends would go into hiding as no one wanted to be associated with the shame. The grieving family suffered in silence, the suicide person's name was rarely mentioned again. It was as if he/she never existed. This was the case with my father's friend who died by suicide. His entire family were ignored and neglected by the very people that called themselves friends. To show solidarity to the family my father paid frequent visits to their home especially during anniversary times. Years later he was still visiting this plot outside the graveyard wall to remember his friend as there was no one left to pray for him. Shame on the Church of that time and shame on those people who became judge and jury in a matter they had little or no understanding of.

Allow me to correct this fallacy; it is not *"sinful"* to end a life through suicide or for a person to abdicate his/her life before his/her life's mission is complete. I've been involved with many aspects of suicide from survivors, intervention programs and healing in the aftermath of suicide. One of the most significant questions asked is, *"Is my loved one lost to eternal damnation?"* I tell them the good news is that there is no hell's fire and brimstone. All souls who die by suicide are met by a loving presence at the moment of impact. They too are escorted to the other side in a light-filled space of love and compassion. From the innumerable messages and information I receive from the other side all souls are welcomed home. Despite the taboo stories to the contrary, all suicide souls return to the light. I say this beyond a shadow of a doubt, not just from the perspective of my own work, but from research available by prominent doctors in this field. Dr. Michael Newton's findings in *Journey of Souls* endorse the view of the soul as that untouchable part that never dies even in those who die by suicide. However, he does say those who end their life by suicide are embraced by the light but they will also be given the opportunity to return again to a physical body to correct the mistakes from the previous lifetime. Dr. Joseph Gallenberger's *Heaven is for Healing: A Soul's Journey After Suicide* is a most fascinating and comforting read. He shares many thought-provoking insights reassuring the reader that there is much help and hope on the other side endorsing the fact that no soul is lost even after suicide.

When you were born you cried and the world rejoiced. Live your life in such a manner that when you die, the world cries and you rejoice.
Cherokee Proverb

Take comfort in the knowledge, and be assured, that any soul which ends his/her life through suicide is nurtured and cared for on the other side. If the soul passed while under the influence of alcohol or drugs he/she will be held in a sleep state which allows time for the essential repair of the soul. This is a state of pure rest and after a period of adjustment the soul is gradually awakened to the reality of their death. The soul is counseled by spirit guides that go through the life review of what went wrong, why the soul lost its purpose and why he/she ended the life prematurely. After a period of healing and restoration, the soul will be shown how to rectify the situation which caused the pain and suffering, and will be given the opportunity to get it right. The soul is always eager to rectify past mistakes and when the soul is ready and if it chooses has the opportunity to return to earth to complete the unfinished soul lesson from the previous lifetime. Always remember, regardless of a person's mistakes he/she is Divine at their core and the soul is always evolving and advancing towards enlightenment.

The Life Review: The phrase, *"My whole life flashed before my eyes."*

The life review is well documented and reported by many who experience near-death experiences as they return from the brink of death. From Dr. Moody's research the life review is detailed as follows. *"This Being of Light presents the dying with a panoramic review of everything they have ever done. That is, they relive every act they have ever done to other people and come away feeling that love is the most important thing in life."* Dr. Craig Lundahl states, *"This judgment involves a review of a person's life and results in their placement in the spirit world."* PMH Atwater describes the life review as, *"similar to seeing a movie, in segments, or reliving your whole life."* No one is exempt from the life review process. It is a debriefing of the life just ended. No matter when or how you died the life review is part of the process. One of the principal tenets of universal law is *"whatever you give out returns tenfold."* Many who have experienced the near-death phenomenon all report identical patterns. That life on earth is one mammoth *"test"* by which your actions and deeds are evaluated during the life review.

> At the end of life we will not be judged by how many diplomas we have received, how much money we have made, how many great things we have done. We will be judged by "I was hungry, and you gave me something to eat, I was naked and you clothed me. I was homeless, and you took me in."
> **Mother Teresa**

The Life Review: Judgment is multifaceted
During the review you will not be asked how much money

you had in the bank, or how many holidays you took, or how many flash cars adorned your driveway; in the last analysis none of that matters. What matters are the little acts of kindness you lovingly showed towards others including all of earth's inhabitants, animals, plants and nature.

Your life review will be shown on a big screen recounting all the behaviors, actions, words, thoughts, deeds and how they each impacted on others in a negative or positive way. When a survivor of a near-death experience states, *"their whole life flashed before their eyes,"* that is literally what they are referring to.

You alone will be the judge of your actions, not God, not anyone else, only you. This is particularly relevant for those who end their life by suicide. The life review provides a platform to educate and rehabilitate, who you are, what were the motives behind your actions, how did your life impact on others, what could you have done differently and what steps you now need to take in order to correct past mistakes. The life review demonstrates that love is the key to all life on earth. How you love and nurture yourself will afford your soul a unique opportunity for personal growth and spiritual advancement.

Conversely, where love is absent the meaning and significance of life can become distorted by poor choices and mistakes can be made. Remember, mistakes are an acceptable part of the human experience and God loves you just the way you are, mistakes and all. Life is about doing the best you can while making the best choices with the level of knowledge and awareness you had at any particular time. No matter what way your loved one exited life there are no punishments, only a self-assessment and learning as to how best to navigate similar circumstances next lifetime around. Contrary to conventional beliefs the life review/ judgment is not made by God or a supreme being, but solely by the person who has died.

Be Light, Stay Light, Light the way for others.
Guy Needler

No Blame, No Shame, No Guilt, No One's Fault

In the Apache language there is no word for "guilt," there is no word for "shame." Our lives are like diamonds. When we are born we are pure and uncut. Each thing that happens to us in our lives teaches us how to reflect the light in the world. Each experience gives us a new cut, a new facet in our diamond. How brilliantly do those diamonds sparkle whose facets are many, to whom life has given many cuts! So when you feel that the rain is no longer playful but harsh, and when the snow has lost its beauty, hold your diamond in your hand. Do not feel shame. Do not feel guilt. Think instead of the way you may now reflect the light of the world, and be thankful for the new cut you have received on your diamond.
Bearwatcher, Apache medicine man

If your loved one ended his/her life by suicide trust that he/she is now free from the pain and limitations that held them captive. Know there was nothing you could possibly do or have done to prevent this from happening. Your loved one could only find peace by leaving this earth's plane. Please do not blame or torture yourself with feelings of responsibility or guilt. Such feelings are soul-destroying, even toxic. Self-blame after a loved one's suicide is all too common and leaves a trail of unanswered questions in its aftermath. Parents, family and friends torture themselves with thoughts of, *"if only I had done this,"* or *"if only I had seen the warning signs,"* or statements like, *"what kind of mother/father am I"* or *"I can't live with myself,"* or *"I should have done more,"* *"I failed him/her."* All these feelings are counterproductive. Be kind and gentle with yourself and stop adding more hurt to the hurt that is already there. I want you to know that self-blame is never the answer and never justified. No matter how you tried to protect and shield your loved one you could not have prevented the outcome. You were limited in what you could do to prevent/stop the suicide from occurring.

No suicide is ever the fault of another nor is it the fault of the victim either. Instead, see the fault as belonging to a range of other factors that create the potential for suicide, mental illness, society, environment, conditioning, bullying, sexual orientation, depression, financial, losses, academic pressures and many more to name but a few.

Usually there are a multitude of problems that leads to suicide, there are no simple explanations. Remain a non-judgmental presence in the midst of the choice your loved one made to liberate him/her from the bowels of darkness. Please be assured, your loved one has found the peace he/she so longed for. The love you shared will always remain in your heart. Love is eternal and that never dies. Should anyone tell you anything to the contrary, they are not enlightened on this topic and are not worthy of your energy or attention. If you wish you can connect with your loved one in spirit. Even if you are not certain how to do this correctly, you can send them affirmations of love or send prayers for the enlightenment of their soul. It is always a beautiful practice when a soul returns to the spirit world to surround him/her in a circle of golden light as this accelerates their soul's healing.

Another way to connect with your loved one is the practice of meditation/visualization. The exercise Creating a Sacred Heartlink to connect with your Loved One is found on page 93. These types of practices can transmute pain into a form of positive healing. If you choose to pray or recite affirmations for your loved one, do not forget to affirm love and blessings for the enlightenment of your own life; you too are a precious gift to the world.

Take a few moments every day to reflect on the preciousness of your human life

Remember that your body is a temporary vehicle which houses your soul. Nourish it with tender loving kindness; bless it daily as your temple of light. Allow yourself to breathe in the breath of life and embrace the beauty upon mother earth, including all of God's creations.

Envision a world in total peace and harmony where every man, woman and child are brothers and sisters of the one light. Trust that whatever difficulties and challenges you may have, the answers lay within your beautiful heart. Open your heart to the flow of infinite possibilities which are your divine birthright. Become a keeper with the ancient wisdoms in the knowing that you are connected to that vast intelligence which over lights this universe. Don't forget for one moment how utterly beautiful you truly are. Most of all remember, I am you, you are me, we are one.

True Story of Gregory: A Planned Suicide by one of my Clients

Sometimes, when all avenues of counseling therapies are exhausted and with a genuine effort to make a difference in someone's life, I am often asked to take on for the want of a better term "hopeless cases." Such was the case with Gregory. He had planned his suicide right down to the place, time, date and method. When he arrived at my healing room, I was stunned to see a most gorgeous handsome 33-year-old man. I was instantly captivated by his brown soulful eyes. In one fleeting glance I knew he was an old soul hanging on between the two worlds. I could see his soul was fragmented as a dark shadow punctured his energy body. I could feel and sense his pain; his yearning for death far outweighed his desire to remain alive. I had work to do as this was going to be one of my biggest challenges to date. I explained about soul retrieval, cutting ties from the past, removing imprints, releasing old programs and basically doing whatever I was guided to do through the assistance of his guides in collaboration with mine. During his consultation he explained he was a successful businessman, had a loving partner, fine home and was short of nothing in his life. However, he was haunted by dark thoughts which were consuming him 24 hours a day. His compulsion to end his life had nothing to do with unhappiness, financial worries, a loveless relationship, homelessness or ill health. Something far greater and more powerful than he could manage was driving and urging him to end it all. No matter how much love his partner showed, he still felt helpless in the face of what he desired to do. Before coming to me, Gregory flew to Europe to visit his family; little did they realize this was to be his final farewell and last visit. After he returned, a broken-hearted partner pleaded with him to seek professional help. It didn't take long for the counselor to realize that there were unusual factors influencing his decision, hence his referral to me. For one who had planned so exquisitely how to end his life, he surrendered without protest to the process as he slipped onto the healing bed.

While in sacred space I called forth Gregory's spirit guides in communion with my own for the highest outcome for his soul healing. After being granted permission to work on his soul and energy bodies I began to open up to channel. Within seconds I was shown two very distinct lifelines, one directly associated with his lifetime just gone, the other his current lifetime. In this scenario, there were two lifelines running side by side with the past lifeline presenting a massive imposing imprint which was eroding and destroying his present life. Immediately, I asked Gregory to take a few deep breaths, relax his body and trust the process. He became an observer of his previous lifetime. It began with a scene from early 1920s. Gregory was known then as Laurence, an English stockbroker, in his mid-twenties. He was fearless and ruthless when it came to financial power and status. Many investors followed his advice by investing in stocks and shares both in Europe and America. By 1930, the greatest financial crisis in history happened, *The Wall Street Crash*. Laurence lost everything, so too his investors and friends. He was shunned, shamed and blamed by everyone. On a bleak winter's morning Laurence was found by his wife hanging from a tree near the orchard.

The trauma and imprint of that lifetime was so entrenched in his subconscious mind that it was driving him to repeat a similar mistake, death by suicide. This overwhelming compulsion was further compounded by the fact that Gregory was now 33 years old, the same age he died in his previous life. With the assistance from my guides I worked at retrieving his soul from the previous lifetime and eventually released the soul energy that was trapped from the trauma of the past suicide. Following the soul retrieval I was guided to release all the ties and cords from that lifetime that were clouding and distorting his thinking in this lifetime. I explained to Gregory that his soul energy remained with his previous life after his body had died by suicide and it was now time to reclaim all his soul parts back. His soul was fragmented between the two lives and needed to be retrieved into the present life. When he was ready he gently got off the healing bed and stood in the center of the floor. He recited the following mantra three times which was channeled to me:

I cast from my bodies on every level of my being all thoughts of darkness that no longer serve my highest good. Today I reclaim my power as I stand within the blueprint of my new life, honoring the magnificence of my soul. I am a living human expression of God's infinite love and healing Light. Today I stand in my power and embrace the richness of life that is divinely mine. I am deserving of living and loving. I ask forgiveness to anyone I have hurt or harmed in this lifetime or any other. I now walk hand in hand in freedom and love with God by my side. Amen.
Mariel

Approximately three hours later, Gregory was sitting back in the armchair, excited about what had happened and proclaimed with huge conviction that for some strange reason he understood everything completely. He also shared, he had purchased a blue nylon rope, had picked the tree and the exact date of his intended suicide. How ironic it was set for wintertime. I am blessed to say four years have passed since Gregory's initial visit and he is enjoying his newfound zest and appreciation for living and life. It is my belief that most people do not want to die, but instead want to be free from the agonizing nightmare that torments them. **(If someone you know is experiencing or expressing suicidal tendencies please help them seek the appropriate help from a certified professional.)**

The following is an abbreviated version of a channeled message I received from a young man who ended his life by suicide. His mother had come to me for healing where she hoped to find some reprieve from her pain. For the purposes of this book the private parts of the message are omitted; the remainder is printed with the permission of his mother. I believe his message is universal and is intended to bring comfort to any family who have experienced a loss by suicide.

Spirit message from a Loved One who ended his life by the act of Suicide

My dear Mother, Father, brothers and sister, please forgive me for leaving you without saying goodbye or giving you the opportunity to try and save me. I was tormented by trying to live and trying to fit into a world where I felt I no longer belonged. I lost myself, and my purpose for living a long time ago. I am sorry for all I am putting you through, something you don't need or deserve. This is nobody's fault but my own. Know that I love you with all my heart and I thank you for being the amazing loving family that you are. Please do not define my life by my death or how it ended. I did not die alone. When I left my body, I was drawn into the most incredible bright light – a being of light took my hand, I was surrounded in the most radiant golden light, many angels lined my pathway and a feeling of indescribable peace enveloped me. I saw many familiar faces and they embraced me and said, "Welcome home." I now start the process of my life's review in my spirit home. I am learning to be stronger in mind, body and soul before I return to earth to master the lessons I left undone in this lifetime. I am learning to nurture the spark of hope that will light up and illuminate my journey back to wholeness. I am with you always – you will find me in the heartbeat of each one of you. I am happy and at peace and know that my love for you is eternal. I love you all so much. Until we meet again in Heaven's place, I am only a whisper away.

Mariel

Part 3: Love and Forgiveness: The Keys to Inner Peace and Freedom

The final part of the book is to help you find sanctuary and healing within your own heart by taking back your own power and moving beyond the pain to freedom.

This section shows you how to maintain a healthy balance between what to hold onto and what to let go. I have talked a lot about love being the ultimate healer of all hurts. If you add forgiveness to the mix you can create miracles in your life.

Insights will be given into the healing power of forgiveness. The simple participating exercises allow the reader to move from victim mentality to victorious champion.

Letting go of the past, finding new meaning, making peace with the past, closure.

There are many inspirational messages that have come from spirit to bring comfort to family and friends. The affirmations at the end of the messages are positive and reassuring as they bring hope and comfort to the bereaved.

Love and Forgiveness = Healing and Freedom

If instead of E=mc², we accept that the energy to heal the world can be obtained through love multiplied by the speed of light squared, we arrive at the conclusion that love is the most powerful force there is, because it has no limits.
Albert Einstein

As I continue my quest for wholeness and embrace the journey of my soul, I realize that love and forgiveness are two of the most integral keys to finding inner peace. Nothing exists without love and nothing is healed without forgiveness. From personal experiences I found true healing came when I learned to first love myself. After years of trying to understand the concept of love I had an epiphany. During meditation, love took me beyond my mortal self and reminded me of who I truly was, a magnificent spiritual being of love and light. When I moved into the energy of love, healing and miracles began to happen. When I trusted enough to open my heart again I was catapulted into the most magnificent spiritual journey where my work had the potential to make miracles happen. For anyone reading this today, I strongly urge you to open your heart to the extraordinary flow of love that the universe has to offer you. As you bring that loving energy home to yourself, you activate your ability to spread greater love and light to all of humanity. In truth, I believe "that love is the real God," it is beyond comprehension, but with an open heart – love can live there. I know this because I have been in its presence. Love was in me and I was in it. I was one with all of creation. Love is a powerful force that can penetrate any of life's greatest challenges. It can bring instant healing to the body, it can send shivers up your spine, it can make your heart pound. Love is a gift that can heal the world if only people would open their hearts to replace all wars, fears, violence, angers, control, and greed, and use the power of love as a neutralizing force to bring ultimate peace to the earth.

Love is a Cosmic Force whose sweep is Irresistible.
Ernest Holmes

Growing up in a rural Ireland, the word *love* was rarely mentioned. Although I knew I was loved – I never heard the words *"I love you"* spoken. In those days love was private, it was shown secretly and never displayed in public. My father always called my mother *"Cinderella."* It was his way of letting us know how much he loved her as she was his fairytale ending. He rarely got angry and could whistle his way out of anything. My mother on the other hand would shout and run a few laps around the kitchen with a sweeping brush in her hand while trying to knock a swipe at the offending child in an attempt to put manners on them. I could say there was a great balance of yin and yang (old Chinese philosophy) between them both. What one lacked the other had and vice versa, bringing a complete wholeness to our family unit. My parents' love for each other was lived and expressed daily through their actions and kindness towards each other.

However, it didn't take long for me to realize that not all relationships work and remain in the energy of love. As a young teenager I witnessed many episodes of cruelty perpetrated upon my neighbor Maggie, by her violent and abusive husband. For years she would take refuge in our home and wait for the storm to pass. I never fully understood why she stayed with him, but somewhere in her mind she believed she had made her bed and she must lay on it. The old church cliché "for better or worse till death do us part." When Maggie died she was finally free from the torments and cruelty that she had only ever known at the hands of her husband. After her death Marty (her husband) became consumed with guilt and remorse. He fell into a deep state of depression and despair. At that time no one felt sorry for him. The general mood was he deserved everything and more that was coming to him – it was payback time for his cruelty. I recall the remaining years of Marty's life were lived in seeking retribution as he tried to right the wrongs he had done to others over the years, not alone to Maggie. While others forgave the errors of his ways, Marty could never forgive himself. Forgiveness is one of the hardest tasks and it takes a very brave heart to enter the vistas of pain and seek healing through the process of forgiveness. Forgiveness will be discussed in greater detail in the following pages.

Love is beautiful, love is orgasmic, love is complicated, love is a gift, it must be nourished. But that is the fairytale; sadly not all relationships/marriages are meant to have the fairytale ending as portrayed in the story above about Maggie. It is a fact of life that in order for love to survive, a fertile ground rooted in trust, communication, sharing, caring and passion must be planted in order for love to grow. The majority of people enter a loving relationship with the best intentions of making it work. It takes time to fall in love but very little time to fall out of it. True love exists when you are free to share your thoughts, feelings and emotions in an unrestricted, uninhibited way. There are no judgments, no expectations just an acceptance of each other's imperfections and learning to grow with them. Whether a relationship lasts a lifetime or a short time is very much dependent on the lessons the soul needs to learn from that relationship. Ultimately, when the lessons are complete there is no longer a need for the relationship to continue. To experience love is one of the most soulful and powerful expressions felt in the human existence. Unfortunately, some relationships descend to a level of punishing, criticizing, and withdrawal, and fall deeply into the abyss of power and control. These very actions are in stark contrast to the traits that genuine love exhibits. Sometimes arguments, critical attacks, emotional ignoring all lead to the ultimate demise where love withers and dies. When the connection is gone and all interventions at restoring the relationship have failed, the healthiest option is to dissolve the relationship. How you dissolve the relationship will ultimately have a knock-on effect on how you grieve the loss, especially if the person dies without having made peace with unresolved issues. Trust me when I say this, it is never too late to say, *"I am sorry or forgive me or I love you."* A two-way communication always exists between the two worlds, all it takes is a willing and open heart to access the higher dimensions (guidance on how to use this method is explained in the letter of closure on page 168).

Love is my divine birthright, love is the energy my heart calls forth, love is my friend as I exist in the vibration of a loving God. Love is the whirlpool of my soul's desire. Love is my destiny. Love is healing every facet of my beingness. I am love in action. I am worthy of love in all its magnificence and glory. I am birthed in the light of love now and always.
Mariel

There is a renowned study by the psychologist Piaget, on a nursery run by nuns in France. The mortality rate was so high that no one could understand why the children were dying in view of the fact their environment was meticulously clean and sterile. Piaget discovered that the children were never touched, hugged or cuddled. They were never held; even feeding was done by a device that propped up the bottles attached to each cot. This meant the children could feed without any human handling. Upon this discovery Piaget recommended that the children be held during feeding times and played with throughout the day. When this happened the mortality rate dropped considerably. A similar study carried out at Bellevue Hospital in New York City showed an unusually high death rate on the children's ward which could not be explained. Dr. Henry Bakwin (1942, cited in Van der Horst 2008) stated that maternal deprivation and sterile hospital conditions to protect them from infections caused the deaths of many of the children. When teenagers were allowed in to play with, touch, hold and feed the children the death rate diminished. Love is the most powerful energy on the planet. Humans thrive on love, plants grow with love, water responds to love and negativity is dissolved with love. Most importantly love is the antidote for healing the heart, mind, body and soul. Love is an energy which carries the living breath to every cell of the body therefore it is only natural to understand how love can facilitate and accelerate healing.

The need to feel love and be loved is an integral part of the human experience – whether it is male and female, female and female or male and male does not matter. What matters is the level of love known and shared. Love is the divine spark within all human expression which creates positive or negative charges within the body. I am a great believer in Lord Tennyson's quote, *"'Tis better to have loved and lost than never to have loved at all."* Being in love is scary, it makes you vulnerable, it opens your heart to hurt and pain. But if you don't expose yourself to such emotions your life may become a living death. Yes, your heart may break and be torn by pain and you may decide not to open your heart again as it is too risky and painful. This is one of the most difficult paradoxes of life, that pain must be acknowledged in order to experience love. If you have been hurt in love it is perfectly okay to withdraw in order to allow time to lick your wounds to heal again. But if you don't come back to open your heart again, fear will sabotage love and take it hostage. There is no life without love and there is certainly no love without pain. I once had a wounded heart and I promised myself that I would never open my heart to love again for fear of being hurt again. With the passage of time, my heart healed and I did open my heart again to the most incredible love. Personally, the hardest challenge was to trust in the wisdom of my own soul. To believe that I was worthy and deserving of genuine love from a beautiful man was inconceivable. Very slowly the desire to love this man and share my life with him far outweighed the risk of opening my heart to hurt again. If you have been hurt by love, pain is the price you pay for that love. However, you have a choice, do you wish to carry the pain in your heart forever or set yourself free to love again? The choice is yours.

I love and approve of myself as the Divine Being that I am; I am the love and the light that I seek. I open my heart to allow love to flow freely to me and from me. I am love, I am light. I am God's beautiful creation. I love and accept myself exactly as I am. I am love and I magnify that love here on earth. Love is my destiny, love, peace and harmony.

If someone you know has died where there were unresolved issues between you which is now causing you pain and guilt, please be assured that healing is still possible beyond the veil of death. There are many techniques which I will use here to accelerate that healing; for example, a questionnaire, a mantra on forgiving yourself and others, including a powerful meditation on forgiveness at the end.

Forgiveness of Self and Others: Forgiveness is a Gift you give to Yourself

The weak can never forgive because forgiveness is the attitude of the Strong.
Gandhi

I swore hell – although there is no hell – could freeze over before I would forgive my ex-husband. After all he was responsible for destroying my life as I was the perfect wife. Sure, what could possibly be wrong with me? It took years of personal counseling, courses and self-help education before I realized that I too played a major part in the drama of my own life. I too had to look at my faults and failings and take responsibility for the chaos my life was in. Personally, I felt to forgive was to forget the perpetrations against me and pretend shit didn't happen to me. No matter what self-help books I read, when it came to the chapter on forgiveness, I would quickly lick my finger and flick onto the next chapter. Eventually, after three years of licking and flicking away all things on forgiveness, my moment of self-realization came when I least expected it.

Early one morning I decided to master one of Louise Hay's exercises. The task was to hold a mirror to my face and look deeply into my own eyes, until I could find the child within. It was difficult to do in view of the fact I could see no beauty, only pain. As I looked closer my eyes filled with tears as I could finally see the sacredness of the God within me. Tears cascaded down my face as the following words fell from my mouth, *"I forgive you, please forgive me, I am sorry."* I repeated this mantra over and over again until suddenly from the very depth of my soul, a presence, a voice spoke and said, *"Today you have set yourself free from all the people, places and situations in your life in whom you had invested your spirit – today you have reclaimed your power, you are free."* At that moment my world changed for the better. I was liberated from the self-imprisoned mind of victimhood to the transformative power of victory. I once perceived forgiveness as a sign of weakness, submission or both. It didn't take long for me to discover the incredible healing power that comes with forgiveness.

- Forgiveness is about letting go of the hurt and rising beyond resentment and revenge to a more peaceful position of power.
- Forgiveness is a gift you give to yourself and has absolutely nothing to do with the other person.
- Forgiveness is not condoning the hurt, but it sets you free from the pain of the past.
- Forgiveness helps you create peace with your past.
- Forgiveness is sweeter than revenge.
- Forgiveness sets you free; no one has the power to control you, unless you allow them.
- Forgiveness transcends all religions and is accessible to everyone.
- Forgiveness is a conscious choice you make to end the cycle of resentment.

- Forgiveness usually takes time; it is a slow process.
- Non-forgiveness holds you in the grip of victimhood.
- Forgiveness does not mean that you forget, it is about letting go of the pain.
- Forgiveness can be practiced by anyone who is willing change and grow.
- Forgiveness of self is the most glorious gift of all.
- Forgiveness elevates the soul.

Forgiveness is not just attributed to holy ones, martyrs or saints but has far reaching impact on those who practice it. New research suggests that forgiveness can benefit people's health and well-being. A study by Dr. Loren Toussaint (2015) found that forgiving others was directly related to less stress and symptoms in mental and physical illness. His study did not imply condoning, denying, or making up with the wrongdoer, but rather endorsed the concept that forgiveness was associated with greater well-being, positive health outcomes including longevity. Most importantly the study found that unforgiveness compromises the immune system leading to many illnesses including cardiovascular disease. As I mentioned earlier, the day I forgave myself and my ex-husband was the day I was liberated from the prison of my own making. By forgiving I reduced the experience of anger, resentment and hate that ruminated in my body. I made a choice to forgive and let go, and in doing so created a new pathway to a more empowered and peaceful me.

Forgiveness releases the past to divine correction and the future to new possibilities. Whatever it was that happened to you, it is over. It happened in the past; in the present, it does not exist unless you bring it with you. Nothing anyone has ever done to you has permanent effects, unless you hold on to it permanently.
Marianne Williamson

There are many stories of profound greatness that have captured the true essence of love and forgiveness. Here are a few I wish to share with you.

Forgiveness by man whose wife and children were shot before his eyes

One of the most extraordinary testaments of forgiveness is written by Dr. George Ritchie, *Return from Tomorrow*. Ritchie was an American doctor who took part in the liberation of Holocaust victims from Nazi Germany. Wild Bill Cody (the nickname given to him by American soldiers) was a Polish prisoner of war who survived six years in subhuman conditions in the concentration camp. Dr. Ritchie was puzzled as to how Wild Bill Cody radiated health and vitality while thousands perished from starvation and disease, yet he was a medical phenomenon as he showed no signs of physical or mental deterioration. What was his secret? Wild Bill Cody entrusted his story to Dr. Ritchie. At the beginning of the war he was living in Warsaw with his wife and five children. One day, the Nazis arrived in their village and lined everyone up against the wall – except Wild Bill because he spoke German and was a lawyer. The soldiers opened fire with machine guns, killing everyone including his wife and five children right before his eyes. He pleaded to be shot with his family but it was in vain. Wild Bill Cody said, *"I had to decide right then, whether to let myself hate the soldiers who had done this. It was an easy decision, really. I was a lawyer. In my practice, I had seen too often what hate could do to people's minds and bodies. Hate had just killed the six people who mattered most to me in the world. I decided then that I would spend the rest of my life – whether it was a few days or many years – loving every person I came in contact with."* This Wild Bill Cody showed forgiveness unconditionally. He showed compassion towards every inmate no matter what race or creed they belonged to; every ethnic group looked upon him as friend. In his eyes everyone was equal. The amazing moral to this forgiving story is that Wild Bill chose to forgive his enemies rather than allow hate to destroy him. In that defining moment after witnessing his entire family killed, he replaced negativity and desire for retribution with love which placed him on the path of healing and reconciliation.

Eva Mozes Kor: An Auschwitz Survivor's Journey to Forgiveness

Forgiveness is really nothing more than an act of self-healing and self-empowerment. I call it a miracle medicine. It is free, it works and has no side effects. Forgiveness is as personal as chemotherapy – I do it for myself. I do it not because they deserve it, but because I deserve it.

Eva Mozes Kor

"Eva: A-7063." This was the number Eva Mozes Kor bore on her arm for life. It would forever be a grim reminder of the gross atrocities perpetrated upon her and against humanity. Eva with her identical twin Miriam survived the deadly genetic experiments conducted by the Angel of Death, Josef Mengele, in the death camp of Auschwitz. Mengele's medical experiments on twins were of unspeakable cruelty and horror, which would later shock the world. Many brutal surgeries and experiments were carried out on all twins including Eva and Miriam and without anesthesia. Mengele's experiments ranged from injecting chemicals into the eyes of twins in an attempt to change their eye color, to sex change operations, the removal of organs and limbs. With the most gruesome act of all, when the experiments were over the twins were given a lethal injection and were murdered. Eva, in one of her interviews, recalled how a set of Gypsy twins were brought back from Mengele's laboratory after they were sewn together back to back. Mengele had attempted to create a set of Siamese twins by connecting blood vessels and organs. Eva vividly remembered hearing the twins scream day and night until their cries faded and eventually they died. From 1944-1945, Eva and Miriam were used as human guinea pigs. Several times each week they would be placed naked on a slab for up to six to eight hours while the most barbaric experiments were carried out on them. Three thousand twins passed through Auschwitz during World War II with only a few surviving the experiments under the hands of Mengele. The fact that Eva and Miriam survived the death camp of Auschwitz was nothing short of a miracle. It was only after the war that Eva and her sister discovered that their entire family had been exterminated during the Nazi reign.

On January 27th, 1995, on the fiftieth anniversary of the liberation of Auschwitz, Eva stood with her children by the site of the gas chambers and the charred ruins of its crematories. Also standing beside her was Dr. Munch, a former doctor at Auschwitz who had been acquitted of war crimes. He wished to sign a document acknowledging the existence of the death camps' gas chambers. Dr. Munch signed his document about the operations of the gas chambers while Eva read her document on forgiveness. Eva said, *"as I did that, I felt a burden of pain was lifted from me. I was no longer in the grip of hate; I was finally free."* She went on to say that before her process of forgiveness she remained a powerless – hopeless – victim of Mengele and that she could never forgive him. Then she suddenly realized that she had the power now – the power to forgive. It was her right to use it and no one could take that away from her. Later it was said by some survivors that Eva was a traitor and accused her of talking in their name. Eva wrote in her forgiveness program that she forgave for her own sake not for others because she believed she deserved to live without pain and anger for the remaining years of her life.

Despite the biggest manhunt in international history efforts to track down and apprehend Mengele proved unsuccessful.

However, in 1979 news that the Angel of Death drowned while swimming in the ocean came as a great relief to many who survived his torture.

Eva Mozes Kor went on to become a renowned ambassador on forgiveness and the truths of the Holocaust. In 1984 she created a nonprofit organization named C.A.N.D.L.E.S., an acronym for *Children of Auschwitz Nazi Deadly Lab Experiments Survivors*. The main purpose was to locate and reunite survivors of the experiments and was dedicated *"to heal the pain, to teach the truth, to prevent prejudice."* After reading Eva's story I was brought to my knees on her ability to forgive Mengele and her torturers. Eva dedicated her life to telling the truths of the Holocaust atrocities while preaching the power of forgiveness as a means of healing from devastating trauma. Eva is a true example of divinity in motion; imagine the magnificence of our world where love could finally cancel out hate.

Eva Mozes Kor passed away on July 4th, 2019.

The Railway Man – Forgiveness Versus Revenge: Most Powerful Film on Forgiveness

Eric Lomax was a Lieutenant in the Royal Corps of Signals during World War II. In 1942, Lomax became a prisoner of war and was forced to work on Burma's infamous "death railway" construction. The "death railway" was constructed when Burma and Thailand were occupied by the Japanese and that piece of precision engineering was built by the labor of over 60,000 prisoners of war. Thousands died during the building of this railway but those that survived endured unspeakable horror and inhuman torture. Lomax was subjected to horrific torture after owning up to having secretly built a radio at his camp. He was stamped on, his arms were broken, his ribs cracked with pickaxe handles, he was water-boarded which meant his head was covered while water was pumped violently into his mouth by a tube pushed down his throat. He was confined to a tiny cage where he had to lie in his own excrement. He was starved to the point of looking like a skeleton carcass with some skin stretched over it. For three and half years he was violently tortured by one particular Japanese officer named Takashi Nagase, who was Lomax's translator, interrogator and torturer. Lomax became the chief target of his sadistic attacks which very often left Lomax with his flesh ripped from his body and left close to death after brutal beatings.

By some incredible twist of fate Lomax survived the war. He suffered immense psychological trauma with flashbacks of torture and beatings which haunted him throughout his life. Lomax vowed to avenge his persecutor and strangle him if the opportunity ever presented itself. But before that Lomax had obtained a translation of Takashi's memoir, which explained how shameful he was for what he had done to prisoners of war. In particular he asked forgiveness from one prisoner, an Englishman named Lomax. After the war Takashi became a devout Buddhist and dedicated his life to atoning for the treatment of prisoners of war under his regime. More than half a century after the war Lomax and Takashi would finally meet again. Both men approached each other on the bridge over the River Kwai. Takashi nervously acknowledged that the Imperial Japanese Army had treated the British prisoners of war appallingly. Lomax carefully read out a letter he had written assuring Takashi of his total forgiveness. Takashi said, *"I think I can die safely now."* For years Lomax harbored the thoughts of revenge on his wartime tormentor. But finally, when he had the chance to act, when he came face to face with Takashi, he chose forgiveness. The story of Lomax encapsulates the power that forgiveness holds in releasing man from the destruction and bitterness that spawns hatred in mankind. Lomax proved that reconciliation and forgiveness had the power to help him transcend his nightmares and heal his wounded soul. His renowned memoir is *The Railway Man: A POW's Searing Account of War, Brutality and Forgiveness.*

Eric Lomax passed away on October 8th, 2012.

His wife had this inscription written on his headstone: *"Sometimes the hating has to Stop."*

Nelson Mandela: Icon of Reconciliation and Forgiveness

Forgiveness liberates the soul, it removes fear. That's why it's such a powerful weapon.
Nelson Mandela

Nelson Mandela is synonymous with the power of forgiveness and reconciliation. He was imprisoned for 27 years for his objection to apartheid. During many of those years he was tortured, made to work long hours in the quarries under sweltering heat, and while there witnessed many of his inmates die after being inhumanely tortured. Mandela was prevented from attending the funerals of his mother and son because he was in detention. Although Mandela was enshrouded with bitterness by not having been given the opportunity to bid farewell to the people that mattered most to him, he said, *"Resentment is like drinking poison and then hoping it will kill your enemies."* In 1990, when Mandela was finally released from prison he called not for revenge but for forgiveness and reconciliation. In 1994, Mandela was inaugurated as President of South Africa, the first nonwhite head of state in South African history. In his reconciliation speech to mark the end of apartheid in 1995, he asserted, *"reconciliation does not mean forgetting or trying to bury the pain of conflict, but that reconciliation means working together to correct the legacy of past injustice."* Mandela's lifestyle of forgiveness, love and reconciliation leaves a worldwide legacy for other leaders to follow in the pursuit of peace and democracy for humanity. In 1993, Nelson Mandela was awarded the Nobel Peace Prize for his exemplary forgiveness lifestyle. While there are clearly historical events such as Apartheid and the Holocaust that one must never forget, as all acts of cruelty come with their own lessons ... best not forgotten lest it happens again.

I forgive you. Not for you, but for me. Because like chains shackling me to the past I will no longer pollute my heart with bitterness, fear, distrust or anger. I forgive you because hate is just another way of holding on, and you don't belong here anymore.
Beau Taplin

The miracle of forgiveness starts with you – when you are willing to move beyond the pain of the past and are willing to take a step towards forgiveness then you are walking towards freedom. Before Nelson Mandela left prison he said, *"As I stand before the door to my freedom, I realize that if I do not leave my pain, anger and bitterness behind me, I will still be in prison."* How many of you have imprisoned yourselves inside the walls of bitterness and anger? Holding onto grudges does not make you strong, it makes you resentful. Forgiveness does not make you weak, it sets you free. Make a choice today – set yourself free.

The Ancient Hawaiian Practice of Forgiveness: Ho'oponopono

This chapter on forgiveness would be incomplete without bringing your attention to one of the most powerful mantras handed down by the native Hawaiian healers. Ho'oponopono is a healing practice of forgiveness and reconciliation which can be used by anyone. It is possible to heal any negative thoughts and negative programs in your subconscious mind by using this process. There is a legendary story of a psychologist known as Dr. Ihaleakala Hew Len, who cured every patient in the criminally insane ward of a Hawaiian state hospital – without personally seeing a single patient. While reviewing a patient's file he would recite the Ho'oponopono mantra, repeating over and over again these four powerful phrases, *"I am sorry. Please forgive me. Thank you. I love you."* After a period of four years all the patients were incredibly healed. Patients stopped being violent, others came off their medication, even hopeless cases were released back into society. As word spread about the miraculous healing modality another doctor named Dr. Joe Vitale decided to learn from Dr. Len firsthand. Their collaboration eventually led to the coauthored book *Zero Limits* which reveals the simple power of these four phrases that can transform your life in areas of health, wealth, peace and happiness. By reciting these four phrases, you begin to clear your mind of subconscious blocks so that destiny and desire can take over which help you get what you truly wish for in life. The Ho'oponopono mantra can be offered to any aspect of your life that is out of balance or incomplete, past grievances especially with people you are unable to forgive, hurts you are unable to let go of. This practice can help dissolve and release old experiences that are no longer serving your higher purpose. By repeating this mantra over and over again you will let go of all the old baggage, resentment and negative energy, thus creating a more harmonious and peaceful lifestyle.

The Four Components of Ho'oponopono Technique

- Taking responsibility for your actions by being able to say, *"I am sorry."*
- Asking someone for forgiveness that you may have hurt, *"Please forgive me."*
- Offering appreciation and gratitude to God/Source by saying, *"Thank you."*
- Showing and giving love by saying, *"I love you."*

I have used this technique very successfully in the past and will continue to use it as part of my daily ritual. Upon reciting this mantra, *"I am sorry, please forgive me, thank you, I love you,"* you are taking responsibility for everything in your life. While at the same time it facilitates the letting go of the most difficult challenges in life. I encourage you to try this technique without any preconceived judgments. Personally, it is a life focus on the innate power that resides within me, rather than what abounds outside of me.

Powerful Forgiveness Exercise

In this now moment I am Willing & Choose to set Myself Free & Reclaim my Power.

You can make this miracle happen in your own life, by taking back your own power from anyone, any situation, who may have hurt or harmed you. This exercise is particularly beneficial to anyone who wishes to heal past traumas with people who are no longer in physical form. Please have a few sheets of paper and a pen ready before you begin this exercise. The very act of writing enables you to release the trauma from your body as it finds its way onto the paper. Be gentle with yourself, this is a process.

Before this exercise please close your eyes and take a few moments to ground and center yourself paying particular attention to your breath. When you feel calm, begin your exercise.

List the person/persons still living that you cannot forgive for injustices done to you in childhood, adolescence hood, adulthood.

List the person/persons now in the Spirit world that you cannot forgive as you continue to hold onto anger and bitterness, even though they are departed.

What advantage is it to you, not to forgive?

Think of a person/persons in the present/past which you have hurt and wish to offer forgiveness to now.

Forgive yourself, stop punishing yourself in this now moment. Think of any situation present/past that is causing you pain/ shame/guilt. Remember there are no judgments, only love.

Are you willing in this now moment to begin to live again and to love again?

After you have completed the exercise, know you can return to this exercise many times until you feel you have achieved freedom of mind, body and soul. After the exercise it is very therapeutic to create a fire ceremony. Burning symbolizes a cleansing and purification process with the very act alone carrying immense power. But ultimately it helps re-ignite the power within you after the process. Roll your piece/pieces of paper and stand before your fire pit, then from a position of power, stand tall in your mastery, make this command to the universe.

Freedom Mantra: Choosing Victory over Victim
(Recite this mantra daily until you feel a gentle peace within yourself.)

Today I choose to set myself free from all the people, places, situations who are draining my energy, controlling my life in which I have invested my spirit. I free myself from the situations of my past; I no longer wish to carry this pain/heartache in my body, or in my life. I forgive myself and stop punishing myself as I live my life now in the freedom of peace and harmony both in my heart and mind. I choose to be happy and live in alignment with God's holy will.

The hardest challenge in life is to forgive someone who has hurt or harmed you at a deep level. Sometimes when death is sudden there is no opportunity to bring healing to the abused or receive forgiveness from the abuser. Therefore it is important to know that healing comes from your choice of letting go of the hurt, pain and sadness associated with that person. Do not allow the wrongdoings of another to keep you imprisoned by subservience. By forgiving you are not condoning what has happened, but you are choosing to no longer carry the burden of pain that has robbed you of life. Forgiveness enables you to take back your power in choosing freedom over victimhood. Remember forgiveness is about you – it has nothing to do with the other person, so why allow anyone to occupy a space in your heart or a thought in your head from this moment onwards. Remember you cannot live happily in the present if you continue to stay stuck in the past. Release the hostage inside of you and let go, seize your power and rise above the pain of anguish; you are worth it and everyone you love deserves it too.

To Err is human; To Forgive Divine.
Alexander Pope

There is a beautifully illustrated story by Eckhart Tolle in his book *A New Earth* which demonstrates the power of letting go and the futility of holding on to what's already passed.
The story is as follows:

There are two Zen monks, Tanzan and Ekido, who were walking along a country road that had become extremely muddy after heavy rains. Near the village, they came upon a young woman who was trying to cross the road, but the mud was so deep it would have ruined the silk kimono she was wearing. Tanzan at once picked her up and carried her to the other side of the road. The monks walked on in silence. Five hours later, as they were approaching the lodging temple, Ekido couldn't restrain himself any longer. "Why did you carry that girl across the road?" he asked. "We monks are not supposed to do things like that." Tanzan said, "I put the girl down hours ago, why are you still carrying her?"

Letting Go of the Past: Surviving in the ocean of Life

Life is a balance between Holding on and Letting go.
Rumi

By nature the human part of you has an amazing resilience and capacity to survive many of life's challenging experiences including the death of a loved one. As discussed earlier not all relationships are founded on love, and when this happens, the grief becomes complicated and it's harder to let go. Whether you were in love or had fallen out of love, whether you were married or divorced, whether you had contact or lost contact, you still deserve to heal and make peace with your past. When you make peace with your past then and only then can you fully live in the present. Throughout my work I have found that many people remain stuck in the emotional vista of utter negativity or total positivity. Often I am given a very unbalanced image of a loved one, seeing him/her as either canonized to sainthood or a total demon in disguise. With these situations it is important to reflect on what you miss most about the person and what you will not miss. Getting stuck in any kind of emotional fantasy can prevent you from completing your grieving process. Hence, the method of closure at the end of this chapter is exceptionally effective in helping people to express and release emotional pain which in turn will bring peace and a level of closure to the most difficult of relationships.

During one of my aftercare programs a man in his mid-fifties spoke glowingly of how he had finally made peace with the death of his wife from three years before. Ronnie had attended my previous workshop on bereavement and loss. The aftercare program follows on three months later to touch base with participants and to evaluate their progress. It was only after the initial workshop that Ronnie had a wake-up call. He said, *"I totally neglected myself by not eating, not showering, not allowing neighbors in, not opening the curtains."* He said he even neglected to feed the cats. It was only when one of the cats died that he realized his wife would not be happy with his behavior. One night, Ronnie experienced an amazing dream in which his wife came through. She told him that she was always most happy when he was happy. She also asked him to take better care of himself, to continue to do the things he loved and urged him take up a new hobby. Ronnie finally understood the best way to honor the memory of his wife was to begin to enjoy his life again. By doing so it was his way of showing her how much he still loved her beyond the separation of death.

> *Do not be afraid to love. Without love, life is Impossible.*
> **Thich Nhat Hanh**

It is important to remember that *"letting go"* does not mean you are reconciled to forgetting about your loved one past. Letting go is a conscious commitment to mourn and let go of the past so that you can find new meaning and new ways in reshaping your life. At a very early stage I became poignantly aware that I will eventually lose everyone I love. I decided then to appreciate the people in my life even more. My awareness of impermanence became the catalyst for helping me realize that in light of death, my so-called troubles appeared not that big after all. It became easier for me to forgive and let go, easier to tell another how precious he/she is in my life with the ultimate truth of impermanence as a reminder for me to be more patient, more attentive, more present and more loving. The final part of the grieving process is when you are eventually ready to *"let go"* of the attachment to the person past with a clear understanding that you keep their love with you. Trust that love is the one thing that transcends time. Even as the years go by and perhaps the memories fade, you will find that the one thing that never dies is the love you shared. The people you once loved still live on in the memories within your heart and that is where love resides. When you feel your loved one's presence let it be a reminder to you that he/she is very much alive in the spirit world, just not in the way you were familiar with while he/she occupied the physical body. Letting go is not just about moving on; it is about you understanding the concept of impermanence and the importance of living in the present, accepting that all things in this world eventually fall away but the energy of love remains eternal. Little by little as you let go and withdraw your energy from the loss you begin to invest in life again where you coexist with your loss and find a level of closure where life begins again.

I seem to have loved you in numberless forms, numberless times. In life after life, in age after age, forever. My spellbound heart has made and remade the necklace of songs that you take as a gift, wear round your neck in your many forms, in life after life, in age after age, forever. Old love but in shapes that renew and renew forever.
Rabindranath Tagore

Closure: A Bridge between Grief and Acceptance
The concept *"closure"* is multifaceted and can be interpreted in both positive or negative terms. Many view closure as closing the door on your emotions and denying that love ever existed. Death cannot destroy love as love will always triumph over death in this regard. I believe that closure is a stepping stone

towards greater acceptance. This means you can channel your pain into more meaningful activities in honoring your loved one. The greatest tribute you can bestow on your loved one is to live again, to smile again, to breathe again, to laugh again and perhaps in time to love again. You don't ever close the door on your loss but you will find a sanctuary for your memories within your heart. Be gentle and kind with yourself as you move on, through and around the various stages of your grieving process. Time has no beginning and no end when it comes to your grief. Closure is likened to closing the chapter of one book and opening another to begin another story. Always remember your story; your grief is unique to you. You may never find complete closure, but you will find a level of acceptance that will bring some form of closure to your loss. Your loved one will always be part of your life and part of your past which makes the concept of closure seem unrealistic. With time you will find a level of understanding that offers a place for your grief, which in turn finds a peace within your heart, which makes life bearable again.

Affirmation: *I Am the Peace that I seek, I am accepting that my life has changed and I am surviving these changes. With each breath I take, I allow myself to live in the memory and sacredness of my loved one. May I feel a golden mist of heaven's light upon me now and always.*

Exercise: Connecting with your Loved One in spirit
(Please give yourself the gift of love by undertaking the following exercise.)

Writing from a spiritual perspective will help you connect with your loved one. It is never too late to say what is in your heart. There are many lessons to learn in life, and it is impossible to master them all in one lifetime. Now that your loved one is physically gone, you may feel despair and anguish at the loss of things left unsaid, dreams unfulfilled, promises broken, arguments not healed. Your sadness may be complicated by unrealistic guilt and blaming yourself is futile. In the spirit world there is only love and energy and you can make that connection with your loved one if you choose. Even if you are not sure how to do it, open your heart in this now moment, whisper your loved one's name and connect with his/her loving energy. In your own time and when you feel ready take a few sheets of paper and a pen to begin the exercise. Remember that in writing you open a channel for a two-way process of communication to occur. Trust that communication does not end with death, and if you have something to say in your heart, know that your loved one will receive it in theirs. It is impossible to bring the loss of a loved one to a close, but with time it is hoped that you find a level of acceptance that will make your loss more bearable.

Exercise: *Before you begin this healing exercise take a few moments to connect with the Soul of your Loved One in the Spirit world or any person or persons whom you feel you wish to share your love with, or anyone you feel you have unfinished business with.*

Take a few deep breaths, close your eyes and bring the image of your loved one/person to mind. Sense and feel their loving energy around you. Ask your Angels to guide you and direct your hand as you channel through the pen you hold in your hand. Your energy now becomes a clear channel for this sacred communication between the two worlds.

Now is the golden opportunity to heal the hurts and pain of the past, and bring about a healing exchange from your physical reality to the Spirit world.

Begin to write: *My dearly Beloved (name), Today I feel truly blessed to be able to communicate with you through this letter, there are so many things I wish to say, but I don't know where to begin.*

The Day you died I was _____

When you have finished writing your letter, put the date and time on it, seal it in an envelope. You may wish to put your letter into a fancy scented envelope or draw some symbols on it; do whatever feels right and personal for you. If and when you feel ready you may wish to burn it; through the burning ritual you create a purification and transmutation process, which helps in your healing journey. You can write as many letters as you wish until such time as you feel you have said all that was needed to be said. Gradually through writing you will bring a certain amount of closure to the understanding of your loss with acceptance allowing you to choose new pathways for living.

We are all just walking each other home.
Ram Dass

Heavenly Messages from Spirit
The affirmations at the end of each section offer a simple and rewarding way to empower the reader with words of love and consolation. Feel free to repeat them as often as you wish bearing in mind there will be some you are drawn to more than others. Also if you are uncomfortable with the words God/Angels please replace them with words that resonate with you – Supreme Intelligence – Source – Buddha – Life Force – Creator.

The universe is full of amazing Divine Beings of love and light that have the ability to connect with many people on earth called light workers, including myself. Having a spiritual/mystical experience is no longer relegated to saints, wise ones or holy monks. Everyone is born with a deep awareness, and a sense of inner knowing. This innate ability is one of the ways that the soul constantly tries to communicate to you; it is as much your divine birthright as it is anybody else's. It is not about fortune telling, reading crystal balls or predicting the future. Being intuitive/psychic is not just something I embrace; it is far more, it is a way of being in the world. It is a language my soul speaks, while keeping me connected to the higher consciousness of God/Source. This is a gift I honor with the utmost reverence and sacredness to be used for the overall good of humankind. Over the years I have received numerous divine messages which are in total alignment with God/Source energy. These messages continue to provide incredible insights and wisdoms for the highest good and well-being for those receiving them. The following are a selection of divine messages gleaned from both private healings and general audiences. Although the messages were directed to a particular person at that time, I firmly believe the messages are universal and can be interpreted by anyone experiencing a loss or who is in need of healing. The messages are about faith, hope and love, with the affirmations being used as tools for re-enforcing spirit connection and healing.

Heavenly Messages from Mom/Dad to Daughter/Son on their Wedding Day

My precious daughter, even though I am not with you physically, my spirit will walk down the aisle with you arm in arm as was once planned. If you wish you can place a photograph of me within your bouquet or within your shoes, that way my Spirit will be walking beside you every step of the way. When you have your first dance, I too will dance within your footsteps upon the floor. I love you always, my precious child.

My son, you are my greatest success – and I am so very proud of you. I may not have said it often enough but I love you. This day is your day, a day to celebrate and make new memories. You have grown into a wonderful man, one I was blessed to have fathered. As I gently fix your bow tie feel my presence giving you a heavenly tap on the shoulder as you stand before the altar of your new life. Let this day be a joyous one, know you deserve love, to know love and be loved. Allow the love of God to surround you every day of your life. May your children be blessed and counted as gifts from the heavens. Talk to me often from the essence of your heart, it is there you will feel my presence and receive my heavenly love. Your happiness is mine this day.

> Message: *My precious child, I dedicate my heavenly love to you on this your special day. Open your heart and feel my love enter every fiber of your being. I promise to watch over you, guide you, and protect you throughout your earthly life. May your relationship be blessed and may true love be the key to your infinite happiness.*

If only I had one more hour, one more day

Please do not dwell on the things you wished you had done better, but rather focus on the journey you shared, the ups, the downs, the good and not so good, the positives and the negatives, the arguments and the making up. Understand that no human relationship is perfect as it is forever a work in progress. For now you must carry on with your earth experiences while other life lessons are placed before you. Know that in time you will be able to communicate with your loved one through the various methods as exercises outlined throughout this book. For now open your heart to the endless possibilities of another world, an afterlife where your loved one now resides. Trust when it is your time to leave this earth's plane you will be reunited with your loved one in a place of Divine love and light.

> Affirmation: *Today I open my heart and mind to the Infinite power within this universe. I pray for my heart to feel healed and my mind to find peace. Today I surrender, I hand myself over to your Divine care.*

Make friends with your grieving heart

Gradually you will begin to draw your world back into your heart. You will begin to feel alive again. Through your senses you will see the beauty in a morning sunrise or an evening sunset. Your world as you knew it is forever changed, but you will find an inner strength to help you through these challenging times. You are learning to rebuild your life around the loss you have suffered. You will find reasons to live and feel whole again. Remember you came from love and you return to love. The love you feel for your loved one can still be felt in your heart. Your beautiful heart is grieving. Be glad for the love you have known and the love you have shared. No one has the words to help you feel better; there are none. People may try to comfort you in the best way they know how, but no one understands the heartache you are feeling inside. Your world has lost its magic and everything in life feels meaningless. You miss your loved one's arms to hold you, you miss their gentle touch, you miss the sound of their voice, their laughing ways, but most of all you miss their physical presence in your life. With the passage of time you will eventually feel gratitude for the time you had, brief and all as it may have been. You will never forget the pain of your loss, but with God's grace you will survive it.

Affirmation: *May the stars carry your sadness away, may the flowers fill your heart with beauty, may hope forever wipe away your tears, and above all may silence make you strong.*
Native American proverb

Continue to Celebrate the occasions in my Memory

I am sorry, dear one, for not being there to celebrate with you all the things we once shared. I wish you to continue to live, laugh and love. Know there are other ways to include me in family occasions, celebrate birthdays, mark the anniversaries, honor Mother's/Father's Day, be joyous in the births, delight in the graduations, light a candle in my name. I will always be with you. Visit my place of final rest, but not too often as I am not there, my soul was set free the moment of my death. My body which housed my soul is only that which has been returned to the earth. I live on in the splendor of God's eternal home. You may pour a glass of wine or a whiskey to honor the memories that will always remain dear. You may toast to a new chapter in your book of life. Accepting that life is changed, and with healing and time, you will find the courage and strength to navigate through these changes.

Affirmation: *I offer gratitude for all the celebrations that once were part of our family gatherings. In your memory, I promise to live every moment of my life with integrity and love. I will lovingly and consciously live my life in seeking greater meaning and cherish every moment of every day.*

Tears and Fears

Tears are the prayer-beads of all of us, men and women, because they arise from the fullness of the heart.
Edward Hays in *Pray All Ways*

Tears can be your silent witness to a loss that no words can express. An ocean of tears is buried deep within your heart. If you start to cry you are afraid you might never stop. Your tears are an outward expression of your deep-seated sadness, and those tears need to be expressed. When you feel like crying – please do so. There is no shame in crying over the loss of your loved one. Your tears are a valuable part of your healing and must be shed. Holding back or trying to control when you cry or where you cry has a damaging effect on your emotional body. Stopping your tears for fear of upsetting someone is unhealthy. Allow yourself time to cry, be it alone or with a trusted friend. Society once viewed crying as a sign of weakness. Today crying is viewed as a sign of courage and strength. Whatever your gender preference, give yourself the gift of your tears which will allow the pain in your heart to subside. If you find it difficult to cry play some gentle music in the background; this will allow the floodgates to open and encourage your tears to fall. Trust that your tears will not last forever, but will lessen as time goes by.

Affirmation: *Today I honor the memory of my Loved One as I move forward in grace and healing light. Help me to find my courage and strength in the people and things that I hold dear. May I open my heart to allow love in, may I open my mind to hear the voice of my Loved One, may I open my soul as a gateway between heaven and the earth. May I be blessed this day.*

Nobody has a regret-free Life – Regrets are a part and fact of life

No one has a *"tabula rasa"* or a blank canvas when it comes to regrets. Regrets will always be part of the pain which can add further complications to grief. Remember, it is never too late to say, *"I love you,"* *"I am sorry,"* *"Please forgive me."* You may regret that your loved one died without the opportunity to say goodbye. You may regret you had not spent more time with them. You regret all the nasty words spoken. You regret you did not show love or how much you cared for them. You regret not buying that special piece of jewelry that he/she admired in the shop window. You regret you did not buy that special ticket to the sports arena or music festival. You regret the times spent apart. You regret you did not organize many holidays. You regret you said no. You regret the suddenness of the loss. You regret you couldn't save or protect them. You regret you deliberately withdrew your affection. You regret the time wasted on silly things that absolutely mean nothing now. Regrets will always be part of your life; it would be impossible to believe that anyone could have a regret-free life. Regrets hold your heart in a vice-grip; it is a cruel torment that sucks the life force from your body. No one is holding any blame towards you – only yourself. Forgive yourself. Open your heart to the knowingness that there will always be dreams unfulfilled in life and that you are not alone when it comes to regrets.

Personal Exercise

Take a photograph of your Loved One in your arms and place it into your heart center. Take a few deep breaths and find the peace and stillness within. When you are ready, say your loved one's name either silently or aloud. Then tell them how much you love them, or you are sorry, or forgive me, or whatever it is that is necessary for you to say. Trust when your heart is open a two-way communication is possible between you and your loved one in spirit. Love is the energy of the heart. Love is Divine.

Create a sacred place to honor the memories of your Loved One

Create a special place in your home that is significant in honoring the memory of your loved one. Place a photograph of him/her there, place a nice scented candle in that spot and light it on special occasions. Place a crystal or ornament that has meaning for your loved one in the space. Create a hanging basket of the most beautiful colored flowers and watch them grow. Create a mural of your life together in picture form, hang it on the wall as a reminder of your journey together. Create a memory box and place memorabilia that are treasured keepsakes within it. Plant a tree in the garden and watch it grow and nourish it with love and water. Support a charity in memory of your loved one which will make a difference in the lives of others. Release some balloons as a symbol that your loved one's spirit is finally being set free.

Affirmation: *Today I choose to open myself up to the infinite possibilities within the Universe. I trust in the guidance I receive containing the wisdoms and knowledge that soothe my soul. I feel blessed, I am blessed.*

My belongings are merely things

Do not upset yourself as to how or to whom you distribute my clothes or possessions to. They do not define me. When you gaze into the wardrobe and see my clothes, they are reminders of how I used to dress and the unusual things I liked. You may wish to touch, smell or even wear an item of clothing to feel close to me, you may shed some tears for a physical presence that is no more. Do not upset yourself in believing that you must sort everything out now. Take time to adjust to the loneliness you feel and the void that now saddens your heart. In God's time you will find the strength and grace to deal with my processions in whatever manner you choose. The things that once were of value to me are no longer significant. From my spiritual home I now know that the true evolution of my soul was based on the many random acts of kindness I embraced; the arms I extended to comfort another, the heart that listened when someone was in trouble, the voice that spoke to defend another, the hand that held the door, the face that smiled upon another, all earned me great spiritual virtue – deposited now in Heaven's bank. On entering heaven's doorway I was not reviewed on the extent of my material wealth, but on the love and goodness I deeply expressed. My precious one, at the end of life *love* is the only ledger that counts within the bank of Heaven. Love with all your heart and soul, and when life fades as the fading sunset you will return home to God unencumbered.

Message: *My dear one, trust that whatever decisions you make regarding my belongings you will be divinely guided. If it takes you months, a year, two years, longer, honor your feelings, and in your own time you may wish to donate my belongings to family members or friends. Hold onto a keepsake or two if you wish, or donate them to some charity for people in need. Whatever you decide know that I am happy with your decision. I send you my love.*

One day at a time, Dear One

Be gentle with yourself; even within your deep sense of loss you know that life goes on. Losing your loved one is one of the most heartbreaking experiences. Always remember that you are a precious gift in this world and your presence here matters. You are not expected to wake up one morning and find that your grieving is over. Give yourself time to grieve, time to cry, time to be angry, time to be happy, time to work, time to rest, time to mourn, time to heal. Love is the center of all life. Allow yourself time to feel the love from those around you. Cherish the memories of the time you had as you grieve for the loss of time that never will be. In time you will find peace as you surrender to the changes happening around you. Letting go is accepting the things you cannot change. Trust in God's timing that you will find new pathways, new directions which will usher in peace, healing and a new way to honor the memories of loved ones past.

Affirmation: *I feel the healing presence of God's Infinite love in my life today. I remain patient with myself as I release all my fears, worries, doubts and uncertainties to a greater power within myself. Just as the caterpillar emerges from its cocoon to create a magic butterfly, so too will you emerge into the freedom of finding your inner peace.*

Does the Afterlife Exist?

You wish with all your heart that there is a place where your loved one now resides. Your belief in the afterlife is not a mystery to be solved but a journey of self-discovery. Your senses have now been awakened into thinking beyond the mind, beyond the conscious, beyond the intellect. You are searching for proof of the afterlife and you will find it. Begin by doing your research into the scientific, medical and spiritual findings which fully endorse the existence of the afterlife. Life is a mystery, and death part of that mystery. For many the belief in the afterlife is as real and as sure as night follows day. Whatever your truth or belief system is, be it God, Source, Allah, Buddha, or Great Spirit, know that a supreme consciousness over lights your existence. Follow your heart into a journey of self-discovery. Discover the infinite possibilities that birth and death are one, with death being another chapter into the journey of your evolving soul. Allow yourself time to read and be inspired by the many books supporting the belief in the Afterlife. You will find comfort as you unravel the mystery of eternal life as you discover that eternity is the true home of the abiding soul.

A bit beyond perception's reach I sometimes believe I see that Life is two locked boxes, each containing the other's key.
Piet Hein

The Land Beyond the Rising Sun
As the completion of this book is upon me I stand here unreservedly in the presence of these pages at the disposal of spirit as a humble scribe floating in the hand of my creator God. There are no words on earth in any language which can describe my heartfelt gratitude to my spirit guides whose guidance and inspiration are weaved throughout this book. My belief in life after death and the immortality of the soul has shaped the way this book is written. It is my deepest hope that readers will find certainty and comfort in the possibility of the afterlife by exploring further lines of evidence leading to the infinite truth – that death is not the end but rather a new beginning, an onward journey back to God/Source. I hope this book presents a compelling portrait of the afterlife based on medical, spiritual and scientific facts that can only unearth and overturn any fears you may have of, "*Where* do our loved ones go – *After* they die?" Some will argue that it is impossible to know what lies beyond death; this type of mindset completely ignores the

ocean of knowledge and information which has been available to humanity for thousands of years. After years of intense research, to include my personal experiences in the witnessing of many spiritual phenomena, I am absolutely convinced that the afterlife exists. I encourage every reader to navigate your own way in considering the evidence and reach your own conclusion. Many of the great religions speak of God and the afterlife revealing that death is not the end but a transition from one life to another.

I have given generous space to my own personal experiences of loss including the remarkable insights with clients who opened my heart and mind to the absolute belief that consciousness exists beyond death. To those reading this book, I hope I have shone a light into the great unknown and given a glimpse of the eternal truth that fills this universe and embraces all living beings: that life is eternal. Release your fear of death and embrace the awesome possibilities that the afterlife awaits you. Remember it is love – not religion – which generates spiritual growth. Love is the creative source of the Universe. Indeed, divinity is love. It is through divinity that all things come into being and all have life and purpose. Divinity created you and everything that ever existed – and proclaimed it good. Love is the powerful and constant source of energy that is available to you every moment of every second without fail.

Although you may lose a loved one, you never lose the love as he/she continues to connect with you through dreams, symbols, thoughts, music and divine synchronicities. Sometimes you may sense or have a feeling of their presence enfolding you in an effort to bring you comfort. As Helen Keller said, *"The best and most beautiful things in the world cannot be seen or even touched. They must be felt with the heart."* Although the presence of your loved one is no longer in physical form, communication still exists at a higher level of spiritual consciousness.

Remember the soul is the eternal part of you which never dies, a God cell of divinity dwells within each individual, which is ever-conscious, ever-existing, ever-new. Therefore, when the body dies, it follows a natural process to return to God/source from whence it came. Embrace your mortality with courage and strength, and in so doing bring in the illumination, the light and power of your soul into everyday living. Choose wisely how you live each and every moment. Strive to make the world a better place for those who will inherit it, your children/grandchildren and the countless unborn generations of souls yet to come. Live from the essence of your heart, forgive others, let go of judgments, hold no revenge, spend time with those you love, walk in nature, show love to all humanity. Be mindful of your soul lessons and what challenges you face in the present here and now. Perhaps your purpose is to overcome anger, jealousy, shame, unworthiness, cowardice, prejudice, to learn patience in the caring for another or assist in a global campaign against climate change, injustice or poverty. Trust whatever you do to make a difference will add significantly to your evolving soul. And when it is your time to return home to the heart of God/ creator you can do so without fear resulting in a most heavenly reunion. May you look at the process of death with renewed joy and hope in the knowing that beyond the veil of death a majestic and beautiful love awaits you.

Wishing you heaven in your heart and starlight in your beautiful soul always.
Namaste, precious one.
Mariel

Meditation: Loved One's A Whisper Away

This meditation is very sacred as it was divinely inspired and channeled to me in 2008 while I was preparing my first weekend workshop on "Loved Ones – A Whisper Away." I later went on to record it as many participants wished to continue listening to it in the comfort of their own home. It is a soul to soul meditation where you connect with the energy and essence of your loved one. I take you on a journey where you climb the staircase to Heaven and meet your loved one/ones in the "garden of remembrance." All the things that were said or left unsaid can now be solved and healed through the energy of love.

I wish to guide you on this powerful journey in the knowing that you are safe and protected throughout the entire process. Please do be not limited by my words or images as your heart knows and understands whatever is true and right for you. This is your time, your sacred space to reconnect with your loved one. You may wish to light a candle, play some gentle music in the background or have a photograph of your loved one close by. Before you begin you may wish to thoroughly read the meditation over to become totally relaxed and familiar with the words and guidance. Seal yourself in a circle of golden light and allow peace and love to surround your energy, space and aura. When you feel ready take a few deep breaths – to begin your meditation.

If you wish you can record the meditation – this may make it easier for you to make the connection with your loved one – by just listening rather than reading. Alternatively you could ask a trusted friend to record it for you.

One final note: If for some reason you don't make the connection immediately, don't worry. With practice you will break through and have a heavenly experience.

Meditation

As you begin this meditation, allow yourself to feel the presence of your loved one drawing close to you ... Whisper your loved one's name, take a few deep breaths into your heart and allow the feelings of love and peace to enfold you. Know whatever you feel in your heart, your loved one can feel it in theirs; always remember that love is eternal and love never dies.

As you breathe in, a column of golden light comes down through the heavens onto the top of your head. This golden light is filling every cell, atom and organ of your physical body. Feel the peace as you allow this loving energy to bathe you in its healing light ... See yourself as a shining Being of light surrounded by love ... and feeling loved.

With each and every breath you take, you are going deeper and deeper into the inner sanctum of your heart. As peace and love surround your body ... you are ready to begin this very special and sacred journey to meet your loved one.

Ask your Guardian Angel/Spirit Guide/Wise One (use whatever deity resonates with you) to move close to you, and gently hold your body with love and tenderness ... with each breath your body is becoming more relaxed ... all tensions ... stresses ... worries and sadness are being lifted from you ... you begin to relax in the energy of Divine Love. Your guardian angel takes your hand and lovingly becomes your travelling companion. Know you are safe and divinely protected throughout.

You arrive in a beautiful garden ... this is the garden of your soul ... pause for a moment and allow all your senses to become alive ... enjoy the experience ... beautiful trees ... light scented flowers ... blue white skies ... as the sun pulsates like a golden diamond above your head ... birds are singing ... and all of earth has a heavenly glow ... Feel peace and joy as it enters every facet of your being.

Your guardian angel takes you to a place at the bottom of the garden ... where a golden archway is placed before you ... hand in hand you both walk through the archway.

The sunlight radiates all around you as sparkles of starlight seal your body in a golden light. You feel peaceful and Oneness with all there is.

Standing before you a magnificent staircase appears, embedded with gold and clear-cut diamonds ... You and your angel begin to climb the pearlescent stairway. You are safe. You begin to climb higher and higher ... with each step you take ... you are drawing closer to the eternal home ... Heaven.

With sheer joy and excitement you finally reach the top of the stairway ... You feel blessed as you embrace the incredible beauty before you ... Your angel lovingly guides you across a white marble hallway ... where numerous fountains and cascading waterfalls of pure love energy spring forth from various places ... you are here in a zone of timeless beauty ... allow yourself to receive healing from the melodies of the waterfalls ... ... See before you an entrance to the right ... gently take a few steps forward ... as the gateway to heaven is revealed ... Here in this place your guardian angel will wait for you until you return.

What happiness enfolds you ... As many beings of light gather round to welcome you ... they gently escort you beyond the gates ... and lead you to the temple of Light where the divine presence of Mother Mary resides. She welcomes you as she stands magnificent in all her glory ... dressed in a mantle of blue ... white veil ... a symbol of her purity ... with a halo of 12 stars adorning her pure head. She smiles upon your gentle face and says:

"Dear One, I know your pain ... I know you have suffered much and as mother / daughter / father / son / wife / husband / brother / sister / friend ... you desire to hold onto your loved ones forever ... remember ... you do ... as you carry them forever in your heart ... in the knowing that someday you will be reunited again in this heavenly place."

In sacredness Mother Mary walks forward and places her hands upon your head ... She presses your head into her heart ... You feel her love and compassion as she tells you ... that you are Love, and from this moment forward you will carry the energy and essence of her love inside your physical heart ... for the rest of your earthly life.

She blesses you and takes your hand and leads you to a place of total ecstasy ... many beings of light gather round you – pouring their loving energies upon you ... you are drawn into an immense light ... you are dazzled by it ... this magnificent light before you ... is the Blazing Throne of God ... You stand before your God/Source/the supreme creator of all that is. Rest here awhile as you are being bathed and healed in Divine love and light.

God/or whoever you believe in speaks to you and says, "I love you unconditionally ... I never judge you as you are my Divine child of this Universe" ... This is your precious time where you are granted a supreme visit to meet your loved one in their heavenly home. ... In the most delicate way God/Source takes your hand ... and leads you onto a spiral path into the garden of remembrance where a reunion of souls is about to begin.

Instantly you are captivated by its breathtaking beauty ... everything you see radiates like the sun ... Allow your heart and consciousness to bathe in this energy ... be imprinted with all you see and perceive with the eyes of your soul ... You see flowers of all colors ... shimmering with tones of golden mist ... anointing their heavenly scent everywhere you look ... You feel safe, loved and at peace. As you stand in the wonderment of this garden ... you see countless family members long passed coming to greet you ... radiating beauty ... love ... and healing light to everyone ... then your eyes awaken ... as a celestial mist looms before you ... out from it your loved one steps forward to greet you ... with rapturous joy ... You wrap your arms tightly and lovingly around each other ... You kiss ... hug and hold each other in this heavenly embrace.

Your loved one speaks to you and says, "Welcome to my heavenly home ... it is from this place that I watch over you and mind you always ... I am so sorry for all the pain and sadness that my passing has caused you ... as this pain now has become part of your life ... Know that I am free ... As I live on now at a higher dimension and learn the universal laws that govern our lives ... I know and believe as hard as it is for you to understand this ... but It was my time to go ... Divine time ... to return to my spiritual home ... the place where you too will be reunited with me One day."

Gently and lovingly your loved one takes your hand and leads you to a wooden bench under a magnificent tall tree ... it is illuminating and pulsating with energy and love. This is the tree of Eternal Life ... where love grows and life becomes immortal ... As you sit together you look through all the old photo albums of your life shared ... here you reminisce on the times you had ... the good and not so good ... and for the lost time now you wished you had.

Within this sacred time you can ask your loved one for forgiveness ... for release of any old hurts ... unresolved issues ... guilt ... questions ... anything ... that was left unsaid before your loved one passed.

Understand, dear one, where your loved one now resides ... they hold no judgments ... only love ... they too are as anxious as you ... to heal any unresolved issues between you ... as now is the time to bring healing ... to find inner peace and have the grace to move forward in your life once more. ... It is never too late ... to say I'm sorry ... I was wrong ... Or I love you ... Or maybe there is something else that is troubling you since your loved one passed ... Now open your heart and feel this heavenly connection to your loved one ... begin to talk to your loved one on all the things you wished you had said and done ... while they were still living ... remember they read your thoughts ... hear your words ... Pause here for a while and take all the time you need ... to communicate ...

Now your loved one speaks to you and answers all the questions that were troubling you and causing you so much grief and pain ... take a moment to listen to the voice of your loved one within your heart ... listen to the messages your loved one wishes you to hear in this now moment ... (pause ... allow time for the energies to exchange).

When you each have exchanged your love/your words ... you both wrap your arms around each other in a moment of eternal ecstasy ... feel both your hearts merge as one ... this connection is real ... allow the preciousness of this moment to enfold you ... becoming one with the cosmic heart of God ... in this now moment ... know your loved one's love is real ... as you carry their energy and essence ... within your heart from this moment onwards.

And now as it's time to leave this garden of remembrance ... know that you can revisit your loved one in this heavenly place at any time ... under the charge of your divine presence ... who will always take this meditative journey with you ...

Before you leave ... your loved one has a very special gift he/ she wishes to give you ... hold out your hand to receive it ... this is a very special gift to remind you of this reunion ... it is a symbol that will keep you both in sacred connection now and always ... This gift is significant with personal meaning only for you ...

As it is time for you to leave this heavenly place ... your loved one hugs and kisses you once more ... But before you go ... your loved one speaks to you and says ... "Please be happy ... live your life ... grieve no more ... as I Am living in Eternal Love and Everlasting light ... know that when it is your time to be called home ... I ...Will ... Be ... There to take you home ... and share in the resurrection of your divinity."

Now ... the presence of your guardian angel appears once more and lovingly takes your hand and leads you out ... past the gateway of heaven ... across the white marble hallway ... past the pearlescent stairway ... down through the golden archway ... back into the garden ... where everything appears illuminated ... brighter ... fresher ... radiant ... creating a symphony of love everywhere you look ... new life ... new energy ... new beginnings ... Take a few deep breaths ... allow the experience to settle with ease in your body ... With renewed faith ... you now know that your loved one ... is only a whisper away.

I wish to extend my love and gratitude to each one of you dear readers for taking this journey with me into the unknown vistas of the universe. It is my dearest hope that you have found some peace and comfort within the pages of Where After. *May you look at the process of death with renewed hope that beyond the veil of death your loved one awaits you. It would be my humble pleasure if you are drawn to visit my website to download my meditations at www.marielfordeclarke.com. Loved One's – a Whisper Away Meditation takes you on a journey to meet your loved one in the garden of remembrance. Alternatively, the Temple of Healing Meditation works with dissolving mental and emotional blockages that cause illness within the physical body. Both provide a powerful and uplifting healing on all levels of mind, body and spirit. May love, peace and blessings be yours this day.*
Mariel Forde Clarke

References

Alexander, Eben, MD. *Proof of Heaven: A Neurosurgeon's Journey into the Afterlife*. New York: Simon & Schuster, 2012.

Atwater, PMH. *Beyond the Light*. HarperCollins Publishers, 1995.

Barrett, WF, Professor. *Deathbed Visions*. Society for Psychical Research, 1924.

Blackmore, SJ. *Dying to Live: Near-Death Experiences*. Buffalo, New York: Prometheus, 1993.

Flammarion, Camille. *Death and its Mystery*. New York: The Century Company, 1921.

Guggenheim, JB. *Hello From Heaven: A new field of research – After-Death-Communication – confirms that life and love are eternal*. Random House Publishing, 1996.

Keane, Colm. *We'll Meet Again*. Capel Island Press, 2013.

Kessler, David. *Visions, Trips and Crowded Rooms*. Hay House, 2010.

Kübler-Ross, E., MD. *On Death and Dying*. New York: The Macmillan Company, 1969.

Lommel, Pim van; Van Wees, R.; Meyers, V.; Elfferich, I. Near-death experience in survivors of cardiac arrest: a prospective study in the Netherlands. *Lancet* 2001; 358:2039-2045.

Lommel, Pim van. *Consciousness Beyond Life: The Science of the Near-Death Experience*. New York: HarperOne, 2011.

Monroe, Robert. *Journeys Out of the Body* (1st Ed). Garden City, New York: Doubleday, 1971.

Moody, Jr., Raymond A., MD. *Life After Life*. New York: Bantam Books, 1975.

Moorjani, A. *Dying to Be Me: My Journey from Cancer, To Near Death, to True Healing*. Hay House, 2012.

Morse, Melvin, MD. *Closer to the Light: Learning from the Near-Death Experiences of Children*. Ivy Books, 1991.

Morse, Melvin, MD; Perry, P. *Transformed by the Light: The*

Powerful Effect of Near-Death Experiences on People's Lives. Villard, 1992.

Muhl, Lars. *The Law of Light: The Secret Teachings of Jesus.* Watkins Media Ltd., 2014.

Neal, M., MD. *To Heaven and Back: The True Story of a Doctor's Extraordinary Walk with God.* Circle 6 Publishing, 2011.

Osis, K.; Haraldsson, E. *At the Hour of Death.* Avon Publications, 1977.

Ring, Kenneth. *Mindsight: Near-Death and Out-of-Body Experiences in the Blind.* William James Center, 1999.

Ritchie, G., MD. *Return from Tomorrow.* Fleming H. Revell Company, 1978.

Sartori, P., PhD. *The Wisdom of Near-Death Experiences: How Understanding NDEs Can Help Us Live More Fully.* 2014.

Sha, Zhi Gang, MD. *Soul Mind Body Medicine.* Group West Publishing, 2006.

Sigstedt, C. *The Swedenborg Epic: The Life and Works of Emanuel Swedenborg.* New York: Bookman Associates, 1952.

Stevenson, Ian. *Reincarnation and Biology: A Contribution to the Etiology of Birthmarks and Birth Defects.* Praeger, 1997.

Swedenborg, E. *Arcana Coelestia.* Library of Alexandria Publishing, 1749.

Toussaint, L.; Worthington, Jr., EL; Williams, DR. Concluding Thoughts: Summary and Integration, Models and Research Agendas. In *Forgiveness and Health: Scientific Evidence and Theories Relating Forgiveness to Better Health* (pp. 289-301). New York, NY: Springer Science and Business Media, 2015.

Villoldo, Alberto. *Shaman, Healer, Sage.* Harmony Publishing, 2000.

Wambach, Helen. *Reliving Past Lives: The Evidence Under Hypnosis.* New York: Bantam Books, 1978.

Weiss, B., MD. *Many Lives, Many Masters.* Simon & Schuster, 1988.

Zammit, V. *A Lawyer Presents the Case for the Afterlife.* White Crow

Publishing, 1996.

Ziewe, Jurgen. *Vistas of Infinity*. United Kingdom: Lulu.com, 2016.

List of Scientists who investigated the Afterlife

I feel this book would be incomplete without giving mention to the many scientists, engineers, lawyers, judges, doctors, philosophers and highly regarded professionals who endorsed the afterlife phenomena. At first they were skeptical, but after intense scientific investigation they accepted that the afterlife exists.

The following are just a few names of those past and present that have made outstanding contributions in the endorsement for the afterlife.

Professor Robert Almeder
Dr. Peter Bader
John Logie Baird
Sir William Barrett
Dr. Julie Beischel
Edgar Cayce
Professor JW Crawford
Dr. Robert Crookall
Sir William Crookes
Professor Augustus De Morgan
Lord Dowding
Sir Arthur Conan Doyle
Judge John W. Edmonds
Albert Einstein
Professor Arthur Ellison
Dr. Peter Fenwick
Arthur Findlay
Professor Camille Flammarion
Professor David Fontana
Dr. Amit Goswami

Professor Stanislav Grof

Dr. T. Glen Hamilton

Professor Charles Hapgood

Dr. Robert Hare

Professor Sylvia Hart Wright

Dr. Richard Hodgson

Professor William James

Dr. Raynor C. Johnson

Dr. Elisabeth Kübler-Ross

Sir Oliver Lodge

Dr. Pim van Lommel

Dr. Raymond Moody

Vice Admiral Willian Usborne Moore

Dr. Melvin Morse

Rev. Stainton Moses

Dr. Karlis Osis

Dr. Kenneth Ring

Professor Archie Roy

Dr. Michael Sabom

Professor Marilyn Schlitz

Baron (Dr.) Albert von Schrenck-Notzing

Dr. Rupert Sheldrake

Judge Dean Shuart

Dr. Bernie Siegel

Dr. Ian Stevenson

Emanuel Swedenborg

Dr. Helen Wambach

Dr. Brian Weiss

Dr. Carl Wickland

Professor Fred Alan Wolf

**6TH
BOOKS**

ALL THINGS PARANORMAL

Investigations, explanations and deliberations on the paranormal,
supernatural, explainable or unexplainable. 6th Books seeks to
give answers while nourishing the soul: whether making use of the
scientific model or anecdotal and fun, but always
beautifully written.
Titles cover everything within parapsychology: how to, lifestyles,
alternative medicine, beliefs, myths and theories.
If you have enjoyed this book, why not tell other readers by
posting a review on your preferred book site?

Recent bestsellers from 6th Books are:

The Afterlife Unveiled
What the Dead Are Telling us About Their World!
Stafford Betty
What happens after we die? Spirits speaking through mediums
know, and they want us to know. This book unveils their world…
Paperback: 978-1-84694-496-3 ebook: 978-1-84694-926-5

Spirit Release
Sue Allen
A guide to psychic attack, curses, witchcraft, spirit attachment,
possession, soul retrieval, haunting, deliverance, exorcism and
more, as taught at the College of Psychic Studies.
Paperback: 978-1-84694-033-0 ebook: 978-1-84694-651-6

I'm Still With You
True Stories of Healing Grief Through Spirit Communication
Carole J. Obley
A series of after-death spirit communications which uplift, comfort
and heal, and show how love helps us grieve.
Paperback: 978-1-84694-107-8 ebook: 978-1-84694-639-4

Less Incomplete
A Guide to Experiencing the Human Condition Beyond the
Physical Body
Sandie Gustus
Based on 40 years of scientific research, this book is a dynamic
guide to understanding life beyond the physical body.
Paperback: 978-1-84694-351-5 ebook: 978-1-84694-892-3

Advanced Psychic Development
Becky Walsh

Learn how to practise as a professional, contemporary spiritual medium.

Paperback: 978-1-84694-062-0 ebook: 978-1-78099-941-8

Astral Projection Made Easy
and overcoming the fear of death
Stephanie June Sorrell

From the popular Made Easy series, *Astral Projection Made Easy* helps to eliminate the fear of death, through discussion of life beyond the physical body.

Paperback: 978-1-84694-611-0 ebook: 978-1-78099-225-9

The Miracle Workers Handbook
Seven Levels of Power and Manifestation of the Virgin Mary
Sherrie Dillard

Learn how to invoke the Virgin Mary's presence, communicate with her, receive her grace and miracles and become a miracle worker.

Paperback: 978-1-84694-920-3 ebook: 978-1-84694-921-0

Divine Guidance
The Answers You Need to Make Miracles
Stephanie J. King

Ask any question and the answer will be presented, like a direct line to higher realms... *Divine Guidance* helps you to regain control over your own journey through life.

Paperback: 978-1-78099-794-0 ebook: 978-1-78099-793-3

Beyond Photography
Encounters with Orbs, Angels and Mysterious Light Forms!
John Pickering, Katie Hall
Orbs have been appearing all over the world in recent years. This is the personal account of one couple's experience of this new phenomenon.
Paperback: 978-1-90504-790-1

Blissfully Dead
Life Lessons from the Other Side
Melita Harvey
The spirit of Janelle, a former actress, takes the reader on a fascinating and insightful journey from the mind to the heart.
Paperback: 978-1-78535-078-8 ebook: 978-1-78535-079-5

Does It Rain in Other Dimensions?
A True Story of Alien Encounters
Mike Oram
We have neighbors in the universe. This book describes one man's experience of communicating with other-dimensional and extra-terrestrial beings over a 50-year period.
Paperback: 978-1-84694-054-5

Electronic Voices: Contact with Another Dimension?
Anabela Mourato Cardoso
Career diplomat and experimenter Dr Anabela Cardoso covers the latest research into Instrumental Transcommunication and Electronic Voice Phenomena.
Paperback: 978-1-84694-363-8

The Hidden Secrets of a Modern Seer
Cher Chevalier
An account of near death experiences, psychic battles between good and evil, multidimensional experiences and Demons and Angelic Helpers.
Paperback: 978-1-84694-307-2 ebook: 978-1-78099-058-3

Haunted: Horror of Haverfordwest
G L Davies
Blissful beginnings for a young couple turn into a nightmare after purchasing their dream home in Wales in 1989. Their love and their resolve are torn apart by an indescribable entity that pushes paranormal activity to the limit. Dare you step Inside?
Paperback: 978-1-78535-843-2 ebook: 978-1-78535-844-9

Raising Faith
A true story of raising a child psychic-medium
Claire Waters
One family's extraordinary experience learning about their young daughter's ability to communicate with spirits, and inspirational lessons learned on their journey so far.
Paperback: 978-1-78535-870-8 ebook: 978-1-78535-871-5

Readers of ebooks can buy or view any of these bestsellers by clicking on the live link in the title. Most titles are published in paperback and as an ebook. Paperbacks are available in traditional bookshops. Both print and ebook formats are available online.
Find more titles and sign up to our readers' newsletter at http://www.johnhuntpublishing.com/mind-body-spirit.
Follow us on Facebook at https://www.facebook.com/OBooks
and Twitter at https://twitter.com/obooks.